# GREAT GETAWAYS

A guide to
fun-filled, scenic, tasty and historic
adventures & explorations
in Southern Ontario

**BETTY ZYVATKAUSKAS**

Random House of Canada

Copyright © 1992 by Betty Zyvatkauskas

All rights reserved under International and Pan-American Copyright Conventions.

Published in Canada in 1992 by Random House of Canada Limited, Toronto.

**Canadian Cataloguing in Publication Data**
Zyvatkauskas, Betty
    Great getaways
Includes index
ISBN 0-394-22247-4

1. Ontario - Description and travel - 1981 - Guide-books.*
I. Title.
FC3057.Z9 1992     917.1304'4     C92-093031-X
F1057.Z9 1992

Cover and text design: Teri McMahon
Cover Illustration: Susan Leopold
Printed and bound in Canada
10 9 8 7 6 5 4 3 2 1

This book is based upon columns written by Betty Zyvatkauskas from 1980 to 1990 for the Toronto *Globe and Mail*. The publishers would like to thank the *Globe and Mail* for permission to use the title "Great Getaways."

## Contents

| | |
|---|---|
| Preface | iv |
| Map | vi |

### *the great outdoors*

| | |
|---|---|
| Cedarena, Markham | 2 |
| Sandbanks Provincial Park, Picton | 4 |
| Rock Glen Conservation Area, Arkona | 8 |
| Pleasure Valley, Claremont | 11 |
| Caledon Hills Provincial Park and Cataract Inn, Cataract | 14 |
| Bruce Peninsula National Park, Tobermory | 17 |
| Be a Farmer for a Weekend at an Ontario Vacation Farm | 20 |
| Rideau Trail, Westport | 23 |
| Bluffers Park and The Guild Inn, Scarborough | 25 |
| Cross Canada Balloons, Uxbridge | 28 |
| Madawaska Kanu Centre, Barry's Bay | 31 |
| Elora Gorge, Elora | 34 |

### *history alive*

| | |
|---|---|
| Crawford Lake Indian Village and Conservation Area, Milton | 38 |
| Ontario Agricultural Museum, Milton | 41 |
| Petroglyphs Provincial Park, Bancroft | 44 |
| Lang Pioneer Village, Peterborough | 46 |
| Fort George National Historic Park, Niagara-on-the-Lake | 49 |
| Battlefield House, Stoney Creek | 52 |
| The Hamilton Museum of Steam and Technology, Hamilton | 55 |
| Sainte-Marie Among the Hurons, Midland | 57 |
| The Meeting Place, St. Jacobs | 60 |

# Contents

## heroes & houses

| | |
|---|---|
| Norman Bethune Memorial House, Gravenhurst | 64 |
| Hutchison House Museum, Peterborough | 67 |
| Laura Secord Homestead, Queenston | 70 |
| Whitehern, Hamilton | 73 |
| Barnum House Museum, Grafton | 75 |
| Stephen Leacock Home, Orillia | 78 |
| Alexander Graham Bell Homestead, Brantford | 81 |
| Woodside National Historic Site, Kitchener | 84 |
| Parkwood, Oshawa | 87 |
| Macaulay Heritage Park, Picton | 90 |
| Joseph Brant Museum, Burlington | 93 |

## tasty trips

| | |
|---|---|
| Pick Your Own Fun at Two Ontario Apple Orchards | 98 |
| Tyrone Mill, Bowmanville | 101 |
| Richters Herbs, Stouffville | 103 |
| Tasting the Grape on Niagara's Winery Trail | 105 |
| Bruce's Mill Conservation Area Sugar Bush, Stouffville | 108 |
| Aquafarms, Feversham | 111 |

## scenic waterways

| | |
|---|---|
| R.M.S. *Segwun*, Gravenhurst | 114 |
| Lift Lock, Peterborough | 117 |
| *Maid of the Mist*, Niagara Falls | 120 |
| The Port Dover Harbour Museum, Port Dover | 123 |
| Welland Canal Lock No. 3 Viewing Complex, St. Catharines | 126 |
| Historic Naval and Military Establishments, Penetanguishene | 129 |
| Flowerpot Island, Tobermory | 132 |

## classic collections

| | |
|---|---|
| Ontario Electric Railway Museum, Guelph | 136 |
| Niagara Apothecary Museum, Niagara-on-the-Lake | 139 |
| Canadian Warplane Heritage Museum, Hamilton | 142 |
| Kleinburg Doll Museum, Kleinburg | 145 |
| The Canadian Automotive Museum, Oshawa | 148 |
| Cullen Gardens and Miniature Village, Whitby | 151 |
| Aberfoyle Antique Market, Aberfoyle | 154 |
| Museum and Archives of Games, Waterloo | 156 |

## flora & fauna

| | |
|---|---|
| African Lion Safari and Game Farm, Rockton | 160 |
| Kortright Waterfowl Park, Guelph | 163 |
| Jack Miner Sanctuary, Kingsville, and Point Pelee National Park, Leamington | 166 |
| Kortright Centre for Conservation, Kleinburg | 169 |
| Wye Marsh Wildlife Centre, Midland | 172 |
| Royal Botanical Gardens, Hamilton | 175 |
| Arboretum Nature Centre, Guelph | 178 |
| Mountsberg Wildlife Centre, Milton | 180 |
| Dorcas Bay Nature Reserve, Tobermory | 182 |

## favourite festivals

| | |
|---|---|
| Fergus Highland Games, Fergus | 186 |
| Black Creek Pioneer Village Pioneer Festival, North York | 190 |
| Sharon Temple Feast Days and Illumination, Newmarket | 192 |
| Wikwemikong Pow Wow, Manitoulin Island | 195 |
| Dundurn Castle Candlelight Tours, Hamilton | 198 |
| Stratford Festival Backstage Tours, Stratford | 201 |
| College Royal, Guelph | 204 |
| Calendar of Special Events | 207 |
| Index | 217 |

## *Preface*

In 1980 I began writing the "Great Getaways" column for the *Globe and Mail*. Knowing about little more in Southern Ontario than what could be reached on the Toronto subway route, I expected to find enough interesting material in my explorations to furnish one article a week for the duration of the summer. To my surprise there was so much to discover that a decade later I was still writing.

What follow are my favourite places and events discovered over the years and over the miles. During that time the range and quality of attractions in the province grew considerably: at Crawford Lake a prehistoric Native village was excavated, reconstructed and opened to the public; the historic Barnum House was restored to tell the history of one of Ontario's Loyalist settlers; reproduction nineteenth-century schooners now sail from the Naval and Military Establishments in Penetanguishene; and a spacious new visitors' centre at Black Creek Pioneer Village provides a stage for theatrical productions as well as a year-round facility for museum displays. As social trends evolved, new programs were introduced, and with the rising popularity of birding, there are now many fascinating programs to introduce everyone to the joys of bird-watching, both in your backyard and in the field.

This book is organized into themes, allowing you to find at a glance the activities that interest you. A calendar beginning on page 207 provides a guide to annual events as they occur throughout the year. The map on pages vi and vii places the attractions by region and county. Where possible I have tried to provide directions that will be useful no matter where your journey begins: where that is too cumbersome, I have assumed that most people will be coming from the Toronto area.

Although every effort has been made to ensure the most up-to-date information before going to press, schedules and admission fees do change, so be sure to phone before visiting. Also, some attractions include the Good and Services Tax (GST) in their admission rates, and others have it as an additional charge, so go prepared. Keep in mind that many of these places are closed on Christmas Day, New Year's Day and Good Friday; again, call ahead.

I would love to hear about your favourite places and activites in Southern Ontario. Please write to me care of Random House of Canada Limited, 1265 Aerowood Drive, Mississauga, Ontario, L4W 1B9.

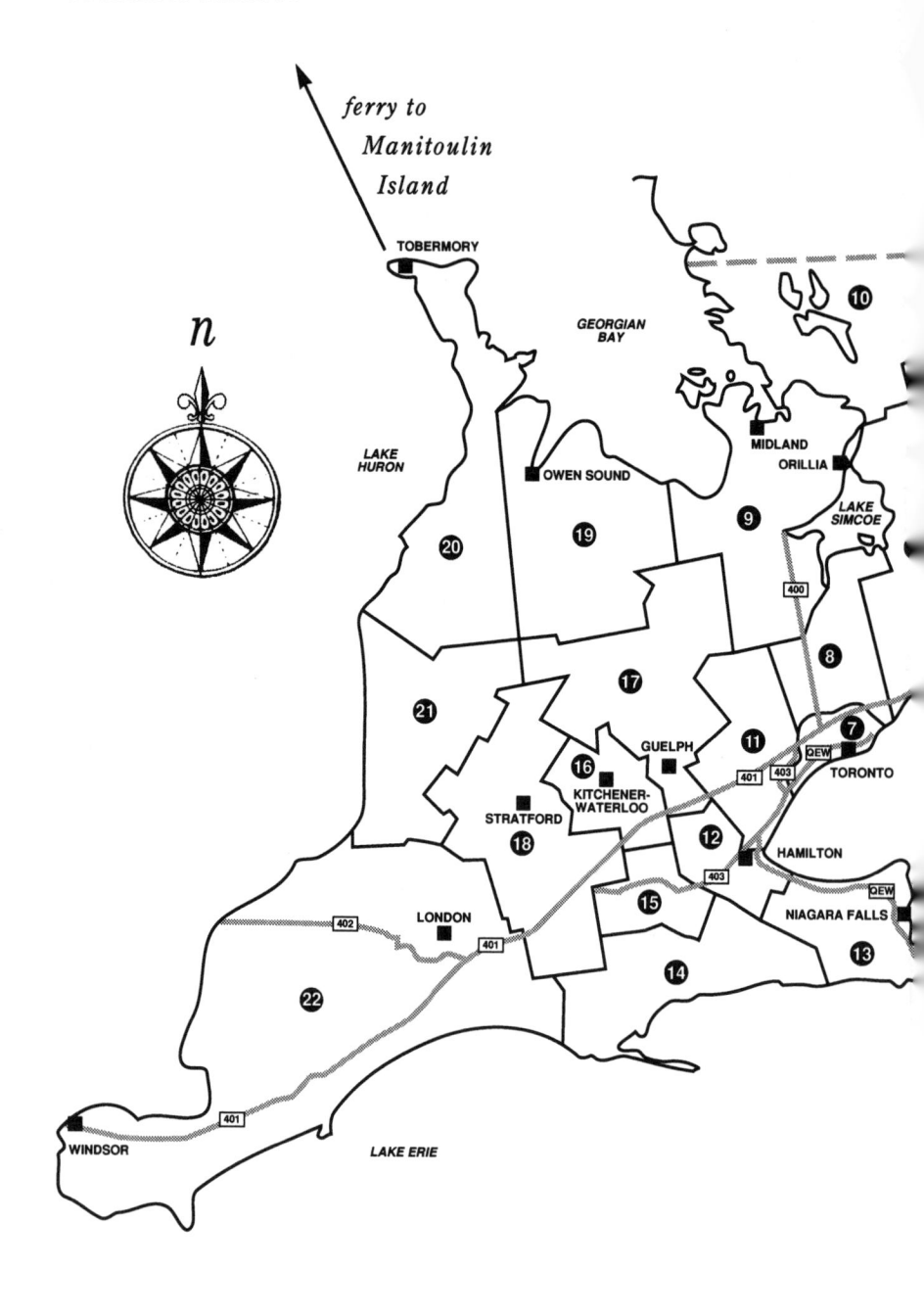

# Southern Ontario

*ferry to Manitoulin Island*

TOBERMORY

GEORGIAN BAY

LAKE HURON

MIDLAND
ORILLIA
LAKE SIMCOE

⑩

OWEN SOUND

⑨

⑳

⑲

⑧

⑰

㉑

GUELPH
⑪
TORONTO
⑯
KITCHENER-WATERLOO
⑦ QEW

STRATFORD
⑱
⑫
HAMILTON

⑮
NIAGARA FALLS
QEW
LONDON
⑭
⑬

㉒

WINDSOR
LAKE ERIE

vi  *map of southern ontario*

## map reference guide

| | | | |
|---|---|---|---|
| 1) | Eastern Ontario | 12) | Hamilton, Wentworth |
| 2) | Prince Edward | 13) | Lincoln, Welland |
| 3) | Northumberland | 14) | Haldimand-Norfolk |
| 4) | Peterborough | 15) | Brant |
| 5) | Haliburton | 16) | Waterloo |
| 6) | Durham, Victoria | 17) | Dufferin, Wellington |
| 7) | Metropolitan Toronto | 18) | Perth, Oxford |
| 8) | York | 19) | Grey |
| 9) | Simcoe | 20) | Bruce |
| 10) | Muskoka | 21) | Huron |
| 11) | Halton, Peel | 22) | South Western Ontario |

*map of southern ontario*

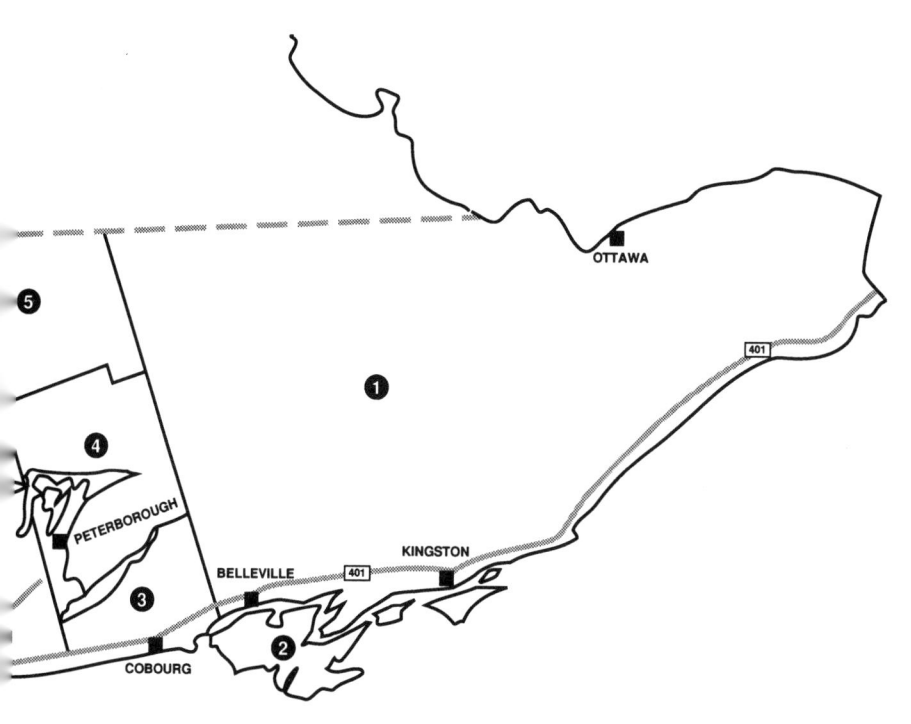

## the great outdoors

## Cedarena, Markham

In a world where the pace of change is so rapid that anything more than a decade old is deemed worthy of nostalgia, it is hard to believe that some things really don't change much.

That's what makes Cedarena such a wonderful place. Although it's just an outdoor skating rink with bumpy ice, located down a back road with few signs to announce its importance, it is a very special place for anyone lucky enough to discover it.

You drive down a snowbound concession road to a frozen field full of parked cars, and it's not until you step out of your vehicle that the magic begins. From the woods, skating waltzes can be heard. You follow the snow-muffled sounds down a little path into a valley lined with large cedar trees to find a wooden chalet and a surprisingly large rink, where a few dozen skaters glide and laugh. Christmas lights dangle from the chalet's eaves, while inside skaters warm up, sipping hot chocolate around an old wood stove.

Despite the urban sprawl that has turned much of Markham's greenery into vast stretches of suburbia, the nearby Whitevale dumpsite that seems ready to burst with Metro's waste and the Ontario government's expropriation of the land on which it sits, Cedarena continues to survive as a community-operated skating rink, surviving on love and a lot of volunteer effort from the folks in the rural hamlet of Cedar Grove.

It was started back in the 1920s by local farm families who found some winter escape from routine farm work by cutting a few figure-eights on the ice. Although a flooded field or frozen millpond occasionally provided some skating fun, folks eventually decided it was time to build a proper rink in a good location. And what a perfect location they chose — a sheltered nook in the Rouge Valley, surrounded by forest.

Local people contributed labour and set to work clearing and leveling the land with teams of horses. An existing skating shelter was brought in on sleighs from another site. Water was pumped from the Rouge River to make an ice surface 8 to 10 cm (3 to 4 inches) thick, and in 1927

Cedarena opened for its first full season. Although it was nearly swept away by a flood in 1929, and by Hurricane Hazel in 1954, it has survived with few changes. The original skating shelter is still intact (with the benefit of added washrooms). Skaters still lace up on wooden benches made more than sixty years ago, and each fall nearby residents still volunteer to clear away weeds and to chop wood for the old stoves that still warm skaters today.

With an ice surface bigger than the standard NHL rink, Cedarena is a pleasure to skate on. The ice is entirely natural, so you can expect the odd little bump — there is no Zamboni ice-clearing machine here.

You don't even have to be a skater to appreciate its beauty. A winter afternoon is well spent just sitting outdoors on the porch bench, watching parents pull tots on sleds while a line of children shuffles along conga-style. Smells of cedar, wood smoke and hot chocolate mingle as you listen to the rasp of blades above the music. In this green and perfect valley you are far removed from the sounds of traffic — even though you are on the fringe of the city.

### *if you go*

DIRECTIONS: Cedarena is in Markham. From Highway 401, turn north on Highway 48 (Markham Rd.) to Steeles, then east to Concession 10 and turn north. Watch for the sign; if you reach Highway 7, you have gone too far.

SCHEDULE: The season is always dependent upon weather conditions. Ice is usually ready for skating by the first week in January, sometimes sooner, and it generally lasts until the first week in March. When weather permits, the rink is open for adult-only skating on Tuesday evenings from 7:30 to 10 p.m. Family hours are Thursday and Saturday evenings 7:30 to 10 and Sunday afternoons 1 to 4.

ADMISSION: Adults $2, children $1.

INFORMATION: During the skating season, call (416) 294-0038.

MAP REFERENCE: 8

## Sandbanks Provincial Park, Picton

With its three-story sand dunes, Sandbanks Provincial Park could be an exotic desert locale, but it's just a couple of hours east of Toronto in the otherwise lush Prince Edward County. This outstanding park features two impressive baymouth sand dune systems separating East Lake and West Lake from Lake Ontario. The West Lake dunes are the world's largest freshwater sand dunes.

These ever-changing dunes were created over thousands of years as westerly winds piled sand across the mouths of the bays. Weather has sculpted the East Lake Sector sandbar into ridges that vary from wetland to woodland to stabilized dunes. The area provides an ideal habitat for many bird species, and each year migrating birds stop over. Birds aren't the only migrants to flock here: each July and August sun-loving vacationers come in droves to bask on the exceptional beaches and sailboard in near-ideal conditions. Although the beach remains the main attraction for most visitors, it's a shame to visit this fascinating park only to spread a well-oiled body on a beach towel.

Campers and daytrippers should make a point of stopping at the visitors' centre, near the main gatehouse in the East Lake Sector. Along with living displays of the local fauna — aquariums populated with assorted turtles, frogs, toads and fish — visitors will meet well-informed naturalists who can describe some of the human history that dates back at least five centuries, judging by the fragments of Iroquoian pottery found in the park.

Staff arrange programs geared to showing families the park's resources. Adults join guided hikes highlighting the park's history, ecology and geomorphology. Youngsters get an enjoyable environmental lesson when they pick up pails and shovels to build their own sand dune system. One of the most popular children's activities is making Native pottery, decorating small vessels and pipes while sitting around a campfire listening to anecdotes about the earliest inhabitants of the region — Woodland Indians who came to fish and hunt.

Saturday evening campfires at the lakeside amphitheater feature a blend of songs and skits elaborating on the Iroquoian settlement and early commercial ventures: fishing, farming and shipping. More offbeat are the spirit hikes offered on three or four evenings throughout the summer, when visitors take a short evening hike along the beach to meet up with costumed staff portraying ghostly figures from the past: Natives and Loyalist settlers.

For a short but pleasant walk, the 2-km (1 1/4-mile) Cedar Sands Nature Trail takes you across dunes, through forests, over marshes and along riverbanks. Signposts along the way are coordinated with a free brochure available at the trailhead to explain how the shifting dunes are gradually made stable by colonizing plants and how flora and fauna adapt to their habitats — marram grass to dry dunes, orchids and mushrooms to the forest floor. Among the well-adapted fauna are clouds of mosquitoes, making insect repellent a must on woodland trails.

The East Lake Sector of the park (known locally as the Outlet) is the site of a private concession, Sandbanks Surf Shop, where you can rent sailboards, sailboats and kayaks. Introductory and intermediate lessons are offered.

Less accessible but beautifully wild is the West Lake Sector, where towering sand dunes form a peninsula separating Lake Ontario from the gentler waters of West Lake. It is a glorious place to hike early in the morning when the shoreline is populated only by a crowd of gulls and the occasional great blue heron stands among the lily pads. These sandy shores are popular with sunbathers, but they are really at their best either early or late in the season when they are for the most part left to the wildlife. Then a boater can come ashore at a spot where the sand dunes are 20 m (60 feet) high and walk across a landscape that looks as though it is rarely despoiled by human footsteps.

Without a boat, you can reach the West Lake Sector via County Road 12, parking in the small lot, or leave your car at one of the neighboring campgrounds for a modest fee, then walk in toward the dunes across a marshy area known as a panne. The panne is a result of one of the more

*the great outdoors* 5

## Sandbanks Provincial Park

regrettable human developments in the area, created when once-towering sand dunes were removed by a local cement company before concerned environmentalists halted further exploitation.

Ironically, even though human activity nearly destroyed the dunes, it was human activity that in some ways created the dunes. When settlers arrived more than two centuries ago they planted all their best land with barley destined for U.S. breweries. Cattle were put on poorer land, where their grazing disturbed the sensitive topsoil, destabilizing the sand that lay underneath. Once the trees that anchored the dunes had been felled, the sand began to shift with the wind to create this sometimes barren landscape. Trees and entire buildings were covered — and sometimes uncovered — over the years.

But nature is remarkably persistent, and slowly the vegetation is coming back. Marram grass is one of the first plants to colonize the sand hills. It is followed by shrubs and vines. Wild grapes are plentiful, but not likely to be picked because the vines are intermingled with poison ivy. Wild roses, cherries and eventually trees such as poplars take root and hold the dunes in place. The dry conditions are conducive to the growth of many prairie wildflowers, including the yellow blooms of hairy puccoon and the orange butterfly weed so popular with the monarch butterflies that migrate through here early in September.

## if you go

DIRECTIONS: Sandbanks Provincial Park is approximately 30 km (18 miles) south of Belleville. From Highway 401 turn south either at Highway 62 (from the east) or 33 (from the west). At Bloomfield turn south on County Road 12 and follow the signs.

SCHEDULE: The park is accessible year-round. The visitors' centre is open daily from the third week of June until Labour Day.

ADMISSION: A vehicle day pass costs $5.75; seniors' passes are free.

INFORMATION: For details about Sandbanks and its programs contact the Superintendent's Office, Sandbanks Provincial Park, R.R. 1, Picton, K0K 2T0, telephone (613) 393-3319. To reach the Sandbanks Surf Shop by phone, call (613) 393-3410.

ACCOMMODATION: Between the park's four campgrounds there are a total of 411 campsites, but the park is very popular so it is wise to reserve early in the season. Call the reservations line at (613) 969-8368. Many private campgrounds surround the park, and there are also some wonderful bed-and-breakfast homes within a short drive. Bed & Breakfast Prince Edward County is a network that includes about a dozen guest houses in the county; contact Jim Boyce, Box 600, 76 Main St., Wellington, K0K 3L0, telephone (613) 399-1299. Rates range from $38 to $50 double; no credit cards. Not part of the network but one of my favourites is The Mallory House in Bloomfield, a large old farmhouse that has been beautifully decorated; contact The Mallory House, R.R. 1, Bloomfield, K0K 1G0, telephone (613) 393-3458. Rates are $38 single, $50 double; no credit cards.

MAP REFERENCE: 2

*the great outdoors*

## Rock Glen Conservation Area, Arkona

It doesn't take a degree in paleontology to discover rare fossils. In fact, many rare finds are made by amateurs at one of Ontario's prime fossil-finding locations, Rock Glen Conservation Area, 50 km (30 miles) west of London.

Visitors to the 25-hectare (60-acre) conservation area are welcome to forage for fossil treasures amid the rocks and mud that once were the bed of a great tropical sea teeming with coral, shellfish and other marine life.

The sea has long retreated, leaving its creatures trapped in a rocky prison, and in recent centuries the Ausable River has worn its way through 25 m (80 feet) of limestone and shale, disclosing the fossilized animals that have been trapped inside for 350 million years. The Ausable-Bayfield Conservation Authority doesn't mind if curious visitors take away the fossils; in fact, they encourage fossil hunters providing they don't take away more than one sample of each species and don't work with a shovel or pick.

Anyone can find fossils here; they are so bountiful that they all but crunch underfoot. Brachiopods are among the most commonly found fossils. These bivalves had beautiful butterfly-shaped shells, which, thanks to the muddy sediment deposited by prehistoric rivers, have remained intact. As the sediment turned to rock under pressure, so did the brachiopod shells; their makeup changed from calcium carbonate to limestone.

Most visitors will soon come across a piece of fossilized coral, either in trumpetlike sections known as horn coral, or little branches known as stag horn coral. Some of the world's earliest fishes swam in this sea, but because their bodies would have been more easily crushed, a fish fossil is extremely rare. After the euphoria of finding the first dozen or so brachiopads and coral fragments, you'll probably want to concentrate on searching for an unusual species, carefully combing the sludge at the bottom of the river valley for any rarities that may have been uncovered by the most recent rainfall. You might come across prehistoric marine snails known as platyceras or trilobites, the thumb-size marine creatures that look like early crayfish. Fossil experts theorize that they would have swum through the water like modern crayfish, propelling themselves by flexing their segmented bodies. Lucky fossil hunters may find a trilobite either spread out flat or curled up smaller than a golf ball.

Crinoids are a frequent find. They are an early form of animal that greatly resembled a plant. Crinoids had tall, stemlike bodies topped with a flowerlike arrangement whose tentacles brought in pieces of food, likely plankton. Crinoids are rarely found whole, but cross-sections of the segmented stem (looking for all the world like Cheerios) are common.

During summer months plenty of people take advantage of the opportunity to pick through the fossil-rich mud, but during other seasons the area is almost abandoned. On a gray September morning I had the park to myself. Try to time your visit to coincide with the end of a good downpour. Heavy rain washes down a new batch of mud, vastly improving your chances of finding good specimens. Because erosion of the soft rocks and shale mud is aggravated by an annual 30,000 visitors, fossil hunters are asked to confine their searches to two riverbank sites and avoid digging.

Rock Glen's attractions are not all in the past. Its river-carved Ausable Gorge and Carolinian forests are home to many birds, including kingfishers, herons, woodpeckers and warblers, as well as a wide variety of trees species such as tulip trees, sycamore and sassafras. A field guide to North American fossils is a must for those who hope to make sense of

### *if you go*

DIRECTIONS: Rock Glen Conservation Area is approximately 50 km (30 miles) west of London, near Arkona. From Highway 402, turn north on Middlesex County Road 6 to Keyser, then west on County Road 12 to Rock Glen.

SCHEDULE: Fossil-hunting is permitted year-round, but some park facilities, including the museum, are closed from October 31 to March 31. Fossil hunters are still welcome during the winter months, providing they park their cars at the area near the main gate.

ADMISSION: From April 1 to October 30, $1 per person plus $2 parking, children under 5 free. No fee after October 31.

INFORMATION: Contact Ausable-Bayfield Conservation Authority at (519) 235-2610, or the Rock Glen gatehouse at (519) 828-3071.

MAP REFERENCE: 22

## Rock Glen Conservation Area

their finds; *The Audubon Society Field Guide to North American Fossils* is recommended.

A museum and information centre displays Native artifacts and, with close to 1,000 specimens, one of the best Devonian fossil collections in North America.

## *Pleasure Valley, Claremont*

Pleasure Valley is a 240-hectare (600-acre) theme park that lives up to its name. Instead of hokey cartoon characters or rides with enough G-force to flatten your face, it delivers simple, outdoors good times. Here you can cruise woodland trails on roller blades or cross-country skis, depending on the season. In summer you can cool off on a water slide or hike across the fields and forests. All these activities are included in the cost of the day pass.

For horse lovers, the highlight of any visit is a tranquil hour-long trail ride through the woods, for an extra cost of $20 (plus GST). No equine experience is necessary to enjoy the outing since patient guides cater to the needs of novices. First-timers, and those in need of a refresher, learn how to hold the reins in one hand, just in front of the saddle horn, and they get tips on steering the horse and controlling its speed with the reins and their feet.

Guides adjust the pace to suit the ability of riders, never more than ten in a group. Keeping the horses in a straight line along the trail requires little experience, since these herd animals already have a clearly established pecking order. Your biggest concern might be keeping your mount from stopping to munch grass along the way. Quarterhorses, known for their patience, make up most of a particularly attractive stable of twenty-four mounts.

The trails cover some of the prettiest scenery near Metro Toronto, passing through a maple sugar bush, pine woods and over hills that provide vistas of meadows dotted with wildflowers. If you prefer to do your exploring on wheels, you can cruise through the woodlands along a 1,500-m (1,600-yard) paved roller-skating path. Admission includes the use of either roller blades or roller skates. Cries of "How do you stop?" bellowing from the bushes are proof that skaters should pay heed to signs warning "Experienced Skaters Only." Novices should first learn how to master their wheels (or roller blades) on the flat outdoor rink in front of the rental area. There, youngsters and the occasional parent cruise to pop music piped in to loudspeakers in the trees. Protective

# Pleasure Valley

knee and elbow pads, which are included in the admission price, should not be passed over.

Although it was quite a novelty when it opened about a decade ago, the 120-m (400-foot) water slide seems quite commonplace today. Nevertheless, it holds plenty of refreshing thrills for those who want to experience the heart-stopping sensation of nearly spilling over the edge over the watery equivalent of a bobsled run as they hurtle down the hill at speeds that make the surrounding woodlands a blur before they splash into a small pool below. Lifeguards are on duty to keep the crowds moving and prevent lingering in the pool.

An excellent children's playground offers some supervised fun for budding Tarzans and Janes who want to swing from cables and bounce on trampolines. Younger children seem more interested in the small petting farm, where they can stroke a goat, feed dandelion leaves to a pink-eyed rabbit and watch a lamb with its mother. A pair of sturdy Percherons take visitors on twenty-minute wagon rides through open fields.

Those same heavy horses are put to work in winter months pulling sleighs. A fresh dusting of snow makes Pleasure Valley seem even prettier in winter, and it provides some excellent cross-country skiing, along 20 km (12 miles) of groomed trails.

For beginners or those who are who are just slow to warm up, the Deer Trail is a scenic 4-km (2 1/2-mile) route with some modest challenges that makes a gentle start to the ski season. And for rusty skiers there are some helpful pointers along the trail: four billboards with on-the-spot instructions for diagonal stride, downhill runs, climbing herring-bone-style and snowplowing.

The signs are a great refresher, although first-timers might find this form of instruction a bit like learning how to tango by following a diagram of footsteps on the floor. Technique doesn't seem terribly important, though, when you are enjoying a jaunt past snow-laden trees populated with chickadees.

Both advanced and intermediate trails lead to a hilltop log cabin where skiers can warm up with a hot cider in front of the fire and enjoy the outstanding view. Special events are often held throughout the winter, among them demonstrations of the biathlon, a race that combines skiing and shooting.

### *if you go*

DIRECTIONS: Pleasure Valley is about 25 km (15 miles) northeast of Metro Toronto, 11 km (7 miles) north of Highway 7 on Brock Rd.
SCHEDULE: Open daily year-round.
ADMISSION: Summer: adults $10.95, children $9.95. Winter: adults $9, children $6. Admission includes the use of ski trails in winter, roller-skating trails and water slide in summer. Horseback riding costs extra.
INFORMATION: Call (416) 649-3334.
MAP REFERENCE: 6

# Caledon Hills Provincial Park and Cataract Inn, Cataract

On a crisp autumn afternoon, one of the most pleasant escapes from city pressures is a walk through the scenic Caledon Hills, roughly 20 km (12 miles) northwest of Metro Toronto. Here Sunday-afternoon walkers can explore scenic sections of the Bruce Trail, but not too far from creature comforts like fine dining.

From the village of Cataract, walkers can enter the Forks of the Credit Provincial Park, but since most folks arrive by car it's best to take advantage of the free parking in the lot on the 2nd Line (1 km/1/2 mile away). In the park, clearly marked footpaths meander alongside the Credit River and up and down hills, connecting with the 720-km (450-mile) Bruce Trail.

It's a beautiful park in all seasons. In winter, bring your snowshoes or toboggans, or cross-country skis for the ungroomed trails. During summer and autumn this section of the trail is very popular; it's the busiest section I have walked. On a sunny Sunday afternoon in September I passed at least four dozen people in less than an hour. Despite the numerous hikers, though, it's still possible to stand at the top of the hill looking out over quiet forests and listening to the rush of the river below. Early-morning hikers may spot deer and rabbits. Birds abound, even during winter months when chickadees dart in and out of the cedars.

Not to be missed are the 25-m (80-foot) waterfalls and the ruins of an old power plant. Those ruins and the Cataract Inn are just about the only reminders of the once-bustling industry here. Fortune seekers first came to the area in 1818 in search of gold, but the real wealth of the area proved to lie in the river, which provided power for lumber and grain mills. Situated at a railway junction, the now sleepy hamlet of Cataract once had enough business for two hotels.

One of those hotels survives, and recent renovations have given it a new lease on life. Thankfully, the renovations are sympathetic to the character of the old brick building. Three dining rooms are decorated in fashionable shades of pink and green. Wildlife prints decorate the walls — and all the art is for sale. Decoy ducks sit on the mantel and sunshine pours through the windows while outdoorsy-looking visitors dressed in plaid shirts and woolly sweaters munch warm homemade Cheddar-cheese bread. The menu is elegant but unpretentious, with items such as ham on a croissant served with apple chips, or escargots in pastry shells served with creamy lemon sauce. The menu changes every three months. Attention is paid to details, like tea from Twinings and homemade mayonnaise.

To make a weekend of hiking, or exploring antique shops in nearby Alton and Belfountain, it is well worth staying overnight at the Cataract Inn, where five small but sunny bedrooms are simply decorated in pastel colours, with cotton coverlets and silk flowers on the antique dressers. Like a true nineteenth-century inn, there are few closets — just pegs on the wall to hang up your clothes — and the two shared bathrooms are down the hall. Terry-cloth robes are thoughtfully

### if you go

**DIRECTIONS:** Both the Forks of the Credit Provincial Park and the Cataract Inn are approximately 5 km (3 miles) west of Caledon. From Highway 401 head north on Highway 10, through Brampton, then west on Highway 24. Turn south at the southern extension of Highway 136 (the 3rd Line) to reach the inn; turn south at the 2nd Line to reach the Forks of the Credit free parking lot.

**SCHEDULE:** The park is open daily year-round from 8 a.m. to 10 p.m.

**ADMISSION:** Free.

**INFORMATION:** For more information on Forks of the Credit Provincial Park call (416) 722-3268 or (416) 722-8061.

**ACCOMMODATION:** The Cataract Inn, 1498 Cataract Street, R.R. 2, Alton, L0N 1A0, offers a weekend special that costs $110 for two people and includes two nights' accommodation and continental breakfasts. The daily rate is $60 double. Breakfast is served for guests only, but visitors may make reservations for lunch and dinner. Telephone (519) 927-3033. Visa, MasterCard.

**MAP REFERENCE:** 11

## Caledon Hills Provincial Park and Cataract Inn

provided for that walk.

One of the most charming rooms is No. 2, with its spindle bed, old-fashioned ceiling fan and a watercolour of pink cherry blossoms. From the window you can see the cedar-lined slopes of the Credit Valley. A second-floor reading room provides guests with a cosy nook for lounging on old overstuffed velvet sofas.

## *Bruce Peninsula National Park, Tobermory*

Of all the Bruce Trail's 720 km (450 miles), few stretches are quite so scenic as the rugged paths that skirt the cliffs where the Bruce Peninsula drops into Georgian Bay. And you don't have to be an experienced backpacker to explore these dramatic trails.

Bruce Peninsula National Park, 15 km (9 miles) south of Tobermory, has hiking loops that incorporate these rough shoreline paths as well as gentle lakeside walks. Any of them can be completed in an afternoon, though a weekend is better suited for exploring all the woodland paths and cliff-top vistas. The Cyprus Lake Campground in the park boasts campsites that are both pretty and blessedly quiet, though increasingly popular. Reservations are necessary from mid-July to August.

Serious wildlife seekers will want to head for the woodland trails. The Cyprus Lake Trail is recommended as an easy walk. It skirts the lake, passing campgrounds, beaches and geological curiosities such as sinkholes (visible in late summer) and glacial scours carved in the rock during the last ice age.

For stunning scenery, don your hiking boots and head out along the Georgian Bay–Marr Lake Trail, which leads to the bay and connects with the Bruce Trail. On a pleasant walk through woods I've spotted hares, chipmunks and garter snakes. Forest smells of fungi and wet leaves fill the air, and wildflowers are abundant along the trail.

When the Marr Lake Trail connects with the Bruce Trail, the landscape changes dramatically. Instead of meandering through sheltered woods, the trail follows windswept cliffs of white dolomite. Boulder beaches are rough going without hiking boots, and it takes some agility to scramble up and over some of the ledges.

The great views are worth the struggle: long stretches of craggy cliffs leading out to the horizon, slapped by the waves of Georgian Bay. In many coves the water seems to take on a blue reminiscent of the Caribbean. But should you be tempted to swim, park staff warn that these waters are not comfortable for bathing until August.

The cliffs that tower over Georgian Bay were once at the bottoms of

## Bruce Peninsula National Park

seas where billions of marine animals lived and died. The animals, coral and various sediments were gradually compressed to form layers of stone. The soft shale layers underneath erode easily, often leaving a harder cap of rock jutting out on top, giving the cliffs their carved look. The eroding effects of wind and water combined create tunnels, bridges and caves.

Even though the rest of the park is uncommonly quiet, this more difficult section of the trail can be surprisingly busy. As I walked farther west, I realized how easy it would be to spend several weeks in the bush — inadvertently. I missed a couple of blazes and ended up trudging back and forth in search of the connecting trail that led back inland. For that reason it is sensible to obtain a copy of *The Bruce Trail Guidebook* (see "If You Go"). I was glad that I had allowed four hours for a relatively short walk of not more than 4 km (2 1/2 miles); the rough walking makes that distance seem twice as long.

While looking for the white blazes that marked the trail, I spotted a brown snake winding through the dried grass. It looked startlingly similar to a massasauga rattlesnake, the only poisonous snake in Ontario. This is one of the few places where the endangered reptile lives and can be recognized by its blunt tail and distinctive rattle. Though all local hospitals carry the antivenom used to treat snake bites, the animal is timid and your chances of being bitten are slim. It is sensible, though, not to put

---

### if you go

**DIRECTIONS:** Bruce Peninsula National Park is 15 km (9 miles) south of Tobermory, east off Highway 6.

**SCHEDULE:** The park and camping are accessible year-round, although you may have to dig your way through snow to get to your campsite in winter.

**ADMISSION:** Free day use. Camping rates are $13.50 plus a $4 reservation fee during summer, $6.50 in winter.

**INFORMATION:** For information and camping reservations call (519) 596-2233. *The Bruce Trail Guidebook* is available from The Bruce Trail Association, Box 857, Hamilton, L8N 3N9. For details on restaurants and accommodations see the section on Flowerpot Island on page 132.

**MAP REFERENCE:** 20

your hand into a dark crevice or shrubbery.

Hiking shoes are essential for a walk along the cliffs, and the strenuous walk is best spaced out in short sections with time in between for sunbathing or picnicking on one of those smooth limestone steps.

# Be a Farmer for a Weekend at an Ontario Vacation Farm

It used to be common for city folk to have country cousins who could be counted on for a good dose of rural relaxation. Increasing urbanization means that most city dwellers no longer have rural relatives to spend farm holidays with. But the good news is that weekends down on the farm are made possible through the Ontario Vacation Farm Association, which lists approximately 100 farms that take in paying guests for a weekend or a week. Farm experiences vary widely and are geared to those who know how to make their own fun.

Rainbow Ridge Farm, on St. Joseph's Island in Lake Huron's North Channel, is a paradise for cat lovers — proprietor Neirdre Powis-Clement had, at last count, a dozen felines inhabiting her barn. She leads visitors out back to inspect newborn kittens hidden in boxes, nursing mothers and prowling mousers who all seem to look with indifference at Neirdre's canine companion, a Shetland collie. The kittens share the barn with a small herd of goats, raised for meat and a little milk, as well as with a few Barred Rock laying hens.

Visitors are invited to help out with chores, perhaps collecting eggs from the coop or milking a goat. Many visitors enjoy taking part in the work of haying. To the uninitiated, the chores can be humbling. Watching Neirdre squeeze a goat's teats, you may think the task seems easy, with powerful squirts of goat's milk shooting into a pail soon foaming to the brim. In inexperienced hands, the same teats often seem dry — until Neirdre offers a few tips on technique. Meanwhile, impatient kittens are meowing for their breakfast. Like the kittens, visitors have goat's milk for breakfast — in coffee and on cereal — before tucking into a heaping helping of eggs, back bacon and bran muffins just out of the oven.

Interested guests learn how to pasteurize the versatile goat's milk. Not just a raw material for chic cheeses, the milk also makes surprisingly good ice cream, especially delicious when served with maple syrup that's also made on the farm.

Education is a large part of a farm vacation, since many urbanites find a barnyard as exotic as a foreign country. Even feeding a goat an apple is a fascinating business as the animal carefully nibbles the pulp away from the core, then spits out the seeds and stem. Just sitting around the kitchen table and chatting, visitors learn farm lore, like how to get deeper yellow egg yolks or how to win ribbons at the country fairs. Visitors can often participate in farm life by helping to feed and look after animals, collecting sap for maple sugar, or other often fun "chores," depending on the farm and the season.

The farms you can visit are widely diverse. At Woodrow Farm in Balderson, horse lovers can enjoy a trail ride. At Chris Utter Farms near Stoney Creek, you can pick your way through 23 hectares (57 acres) of orchards and berry patches. Ontario farmers, it seems, raise just about everything from llamas to pheasants. The accommodations, too, are diverse, ranging from rustic to luxurious. Some of the more trendy homes boast waterbeds and hot tubs; others are old homes lived in by generations of the same farm family. Some offer bedrooms in the family home, others offer separate apartments or cottages. One of the more luxurious is Blueroof Farm, with a fascinating history dating back to the War of 1812, during which its first proprietor was killed; his widow went on to pioneer the land. Today it offers sumptuous accommodation, gourmet meals and a private nature reserve where you can wander trails past ponds and maple woods. Even amid the luxury, though, guests are cordially invited to lend a hand with

*if you go*

The Ontario Ministry of Tourism and Recreation publishes a free listing of nearly 100 participating farms, complete with brief descriptions, in its booklet *Alternative Accommodations*, available at Ontario Travel offices, or call 965-4008 from the Toronto area, 1-800-ONT-ARIO outside the Toronto area. The Ontario Vacation Farm Association, R.R. 2, Alma, N0B 1A0, is a self-regulated organization and members are inspected regularly.

SCHEDULE: Some farms, although not all, are open year-round.

COST: Prices generally range from about $35 to $60 double for an overnight stay, including breakfast: a few are higher. Expect to pay more for a separate cottage or apartment.

## Be a Farmer for a Weekend at an Ontario Vacation Farm

the dishes. Because of the wide range, it's a good idea to ask lots of questions about the facilities before you make a booking.

Most farms provide hearty breakfasts, and a few will provide other meals. Farm hosts can usually offer some good tips on area attractions. Many keep a stack of brochures for curious guests.

## Rideau Trail, Westport

Although it starts and ends in two major cities — Kingston and Ottawa — crossing some very attractive scenery in between, the Rideau Trail is probably one of the best-kept secrets in Ontario. This scenic hiking route meanders through farmland, forest, marsh and meadow, covering a great variety of terrain from rugged Canadian Shield to gentle grazing pastures with nearly 400 km (250 miles) (including numerous side loops) of well-marked paths from a Kingston park to the nation's capital.

It is also a trail with some interesting history. Natives and fur traders had long used the route that was, about 1812, proposed as a passage for military craft between Kingston and Montreal. For the route to be navigated by military craft, dams and locks would be needed, and in 1819 the Duke of Richmond, then governor-in-chief of British North America, slogged along these backwoods routes to investigate their potential. Although he successfully completed the trek, thereby becoming the first recorded Rideau Trail hiker, the trip proved tragic for him: the duke contracted rabies after he was bitten by a pet fox.

Modern-day hikers have it much easier, since the trail passes through many towns and parks with a wide range of facilities. It is possible to spend the better part of a summer hiking the trail in one long journey, like the duke, camping overnight at sites that range from primitive at Gould Lake, where hikers can explore abandoned mica mine pits, to luxurious at Frontenac Provincial Park, where campgrounds come complete with showers. The trail itself is well marked by volunteers who have put bright orange triangles (all pointing toward Kingston) on hydro poles and trees or painted them on rocks.

For a weekend trip it makes sense to find a base like one of the bed-and-breakfasts in the pretty village of Westport. Situated at the western end of Upper Rideau Lake, the village was once a port on the Rideau Canal steamer route. A booming mill town in the early 1800s, it sank into decline when commercial traffic dropped off later in the century. In recent years it has been discovered by tourists and artists who are

## Rideau Trail

delighted with its nineteenth-century streetscapes and pretty views of the lake. One of the best-known B&Bs here is The Cove, an all-season inn beautifully situated on the waterfront and decorated in Victorian style with many old furnishings from the Château Laurier hotel.

From Westport hikers can climb to the top of Foley Mountain, the highest point on the trail at 207 m (680 feet) above sea level. More slothful souls may choose to drive, following County Road 10 north out of town as it winds up a steep granite cliff to Foley Mountain Conservation Area, a great place for a picnic with a view.

### if you go

**DIRECTIONS:** Westport is approximately 50 km (30 miles) north of Kingston via Frontenac County Road 10.

**SCHEDULE:** The trail is accessible year-round and is sometimes used by cross-country skiers.

**ADMISSION:** There is no charge to hike the trail. Hikers should be equipped with proper hiking boots, water bottle and hiking gear. A pocket-size copy of *The Rideau Trail book* is essential for any serious walker; it is available through many outdoor stores for about $23 or through The Rideau Trail Association, Box 15, Kingston, K7L 4V6.

**INFORMATION:** The Ottawa branch of the Rideau Trail Club is very active, and anyone who calls their number, (613) 567-2229, will hear a taped description of upcoming hikes and outings along the Ottawa end of the trail. Guided hikes and ski trips are offered throughout the year.

For information about the Kingston end of the trail call (613) 545-0823.

**ACCOMMODATION:** The Cove, Westport, K0G 1X0, charges $50 to $90 double, including a full breakfast. The rate goes up by $10 a night during July and August. Telephone (613) 273-3636. Visa, MasterCard.

**MAP REFERENCE:** 1

## Bluffers Park and The Guild Inn, Scarborough

To those who don't know Scarborough, the thought of a day here sounds about as enjoyable as a sentence to the Gulag. No wonder. Those poorly planned stretches of used-car lots, ugly strip plazas and discount outlets earn the place the popular epithet of Scarberia. But there is another side to Scarborough that is strikingly beautiful: sculpture gardens and windswept bluffs.

It was the bluffs that gave Scarborough its name. In the nineteenth century Elizabeth Simcoe, wife of Governor John Simcoe, was reminded of the chalky white cliffs of her native Yorkshire hometown, and so brought the name to the new world. Definitely the city's most dramatic geological feature, these weather-worn slopes dominate a 15-km (9-mile) stretch of Lake Ontario shoreline.

To reach the base of the bluffs, drive south on Brimley Rd. to Bluffers Park, a surprisingly beautiful park designed to prevent further erosion of the bluffs and damage to the pricey real estate on top by sheltering them from the full force of Lake Ontario's waves. A massive mudslide that closed the only road to the park for six weeks in the spring of 1991 is proof that the bluffs will persist in their protean transformations, asserting their ever-changing form through erosion. Construction in the park has been done with a great deal of sensitivity to the natural beauty of the bluffs, with even the public washrooms echoing their Gothic forms.

This is a great park for combing some of the city's quietest beaches or spotting shorebirds, especially migrating geese and ducks in the fall and spring. From the foot of the cliffs the sounds of Scarborough's steets are lost in the lapping waves and the cries of seabirds that seek shelter in the manmade harbour. A blissful afternoon can be spent watching the sailboats that moor here, feeding bread crusts to geese or just skipping stones on the water. Avid fishermen can usually find charter boats operating out of the harbour that will take parties on fishing excursions to catch the salmon that frequent the area.

While Bluffers Park offers outstanding views from the bottom of the

## Bluffers Park and The Guild Inn

bluffs, to enjoy them from above, head farther east along Kingston Rd. to Scarborough's retreat, The Guild Inn. This lakeside property, owned by Metro but currently operated by the same people who peddle hot dogs in Toronto's domed stadium, dates back to 1932 when, in the midst of the Depression, Rosa and Spencer Clark decided to help artists and artisans by creating a place where they could work and earn a livelihood.

Set in beautiful woodlands at the top of the Scarborough Bluffs, the inn soon attracted numerous visitors. Before long the hotel began to grow. By the 1950s Metropolitan Toronto had expanded to encompass the 160-hectare (400-acre) property within its boundaries. Most of the land was sold off to pay taxes, and today the inn sits on an attractive parklike site surrounded by woods, gardens and a unique collection of sculpture known as the Spencer Clark Collection of Historic Architecture. Many of the unusual pieces were salvaged from buildings long ago demolished. Ionic columns and pieces of bas relief that once graced Toronto's great buildings are a sad but eloquent testimony to the memorable architecture lost in the city's eager rush to rebuild a downtown core with boring blocks of glass-sheathed office towers. Many architectural fragments have been reassembled with a note of whimsy — most notably the pillars of the old Bank of Toronto as a Greek theatre.

Several historic cottages hidden in the woods are still used as artists' studios. Particularly attractive is a wooden cabin whose eaves are embellished with carved dragons and whose door is guarded by two helmeted wooden Viking heads. Set among the trees, it looks as if it belongs in a Grimm Brothers' fairy tale. Visitors are welcome to tour many of the studios.

Inside, The Guild Inn looks much like an attractive old English club, with lots of wood paneling — a reminder of the days when craftsmen first worked here. The unusual dining-room chairs are also a reminder of those days. Each is adorned with hand-carved horse heads. Hallways are filled with antique sideboards, assorted pieces of sculpture and glass cases full of old teacups. Guest rooms are still in service and retain such charming details as hand-carved lamps alongside the aging plumbing and radiators. Modern rooms in the new wing are more spacious and tend to have better views, particularly on the lake side.

## if you go

DIRECTIONS: Bluffers Park is at the south end of Brimley Rd., south off Kingston Rd. in Scarborough.

SCHEDULE: Open daily year-round.

ADMISSION: Free.

INFORMATION: Call Metro Parks at (416) 392-8186.

ACCOMMODATION/DINING: The Guild Inn is at 201 Guildwood Parkway, Scarborough, M1E 1P6, telephone (416) 261-3331. Sunday brunch is a local institution, so reserve in advance; $21.95 per person. Visa, MasterCard, Amex, EnRoute, Diners Club. Room rates range from $69 to $120, depending on the season and type of room. A $99 Country Classic Getaway package offers overnight accommodation with dinner and breakfast for two. The public may tour the grounds for free.

MAP REFERENCE: 7

## Cross Canada Balloons, Uxbridge

There is probably no better way to see the fall colours than from a hot-air balloon. At 300 m (1,000 feet) above the ground, the view is spectacular. There's no greasy glass to blur the crisp air and no tall buildings to block the view. Today this fast-growing sport is easily enjoyed by novices, who can sample the joys of ballooning with any of several balloon companies around Metro, such as Cross Canada Balloons, near Uxbridge.

Ballooning is safest when the air is still — at dusk and dawn. So in the predawn hours of Sunday morning bleary-eyed drivers still wishing for a second cup of coffee make their way northeast of Metro to the appointed launch site. These sites vary according to wind conditions, though on a calm morning the crew will lift off from balloonist Michael Cross's home base near Stouffville.

Passengers are promptly put to work helping to ready the balloons for launching. First the crew unpacks the nylon envelopes — the proper term for the colourful inflatable part of the balloon — and spreads them on the dewy grass while securing them to wicker baskets lying on their sides.

Jets of flame from propane burners create the hot air while balloons are in the air, but on the ground a massive fan is needed to inflate the envelope with cold air. Passengers help by holding open the mouth of the balloon until it is sufficiently inflated to float upright. Then they quickly hop into the basket, ready for takeoff.

With little ceremony, the passenger-laden baskets are soon rising high above the field. In a couple of minutes the balloons are 200 m (650 feet) above the ground, affording a view of the countryside rolling away in the morning mists. The balloon gains altitude surprisingly quickly. According to Michael Cross, a lift of 500 m (1,700 feet) per minute is possible, although balloon pilots stick to the safer rate of 100 m (330 feet) per minute. Even so, passengers will likely notice their ears popping.

Although steering is not possible, one thing the balloonist can control is altitude. Turning on the gas flame heats up the air inside the balloon and sends it higher; pulling a rope that opens a vent at the top of the balloon lets out hot air to cause descent. Winds are generally faster higher up, so by lowering altitude the balloon can usually be slowed down.

Ballooning is a sport that appeals to the naturally nosy personality. One of the greatest pleasures I found was the view of country estates that are obscured at ground level by trees and fences. Balloonists can peek into the backyards of elegant country mansions to snoop at tennis courts, private air strips and swimming pools.

A balloon 23 m (75 feet) tall attracts attention, as does the powerful hiss of the propane burner. As it drifts over fields, herds of cows scatter, dogs bark and their owners — often still clad in pajamas — come outside to investigate. Pedestrians in small towns shout greetings to the balloon, and their cries carry so clearly in the early-morning air that they sound close by, even though they're difficult to spot hundreds of meters below.

It is especially enjoyable to go up in the company of another balloon. When they travel together each rises and falls to maintain roughly the same speed as the other. The lower altitudes are just as enjoyable as the high panoramas, as you brush past the treetops and look for wildlife in the rosy light of early morning.

The distance traveled depends upon winds, but after about an hour and 20 minutes the balloonist usually begins to look for a landing spot, preferably somewhere flat and hard that is out of the way of crops and animals. All the while, a crewmember in a pickup truck follows the balloon on the roads below, ready to ferry

### *if you go*

**DIRECTIONS:** Cross Canada Balloons is on Davis Dr., northwest of Uxbridge. From Highway 404, take the Davis Dr. exit east for 20 km (12 miles).

**SCHEDULE:** Ballooning is possible year-round, but autumn is an especially good season for the sport, not only for the colours but because the cooler air is more stable. Flights vary in length from 60 to 90 minutes, depending on the winds.

**COST:** $125 to $200 per person, depending on the number of passengers. No credit cards.

**Information:** Contact Cross Canada Balloons, Box 114, Goodwood, L0C 1A0, telephone (416) 852-6055.

**MAP REFERENCE:** 6

## Cross Canada Balloons

passengers back to home base for a celebratory glass of bubbly.

Touchdowns vary with conditions, but usually all you'll feel is a couple of bumps and a bit of dragging before coming to rest — not much worse than some airplane landings I've experienced. Within minutes curious onlookers usually come by to inspect the colourful balloon slowly deflating in the field.

## Madawaska Kanu Centre, Barry's Bay

Even if you've never seen a real kayak, chances are you'll be doing Eskimo rolls in one by the time you finish a weekend at the Madawaska Kanu Centre. This canoe and kayak school, southeast of Algonquin Park, caters to both seasoned canoeists who want a little practice and polish before heading out on a difficult trip as well as to kayaking students at all levels, from total novice to advanced. But it is kayaking that is the centre's main focus.

Guests arrive on Friday evenings (pickup can be arranged to meet the Voyageur bus in Barry's Bay) after dinner and settle in for an evening of videos showing paddlers everywhere from Iceland to the Nahanni. It helps set the mood for Saturday morning, when, after an ample homecooked breakfast, would-be kayakers rendezvous on the dock ready to paddle, attired in bathing suits, running shoes and possibly polypropylene underwear. The camp rents life jackets, helmets, paddles, spray skirts and wetsuits.

Although a weekend party may number thirty to forty people, come instruction time the group breaks down into small classes, no more than five kayakers per instructor. Novices first dip their paddles in calm, flat water. Since falling out of the craft is invariably the biggest anxiety facing new kayakers, the school staff believe novices should get this fear out of their system right off the bat. So they start the day with a "wet exit" done by leaning forward to somersault out of the kayak. Students soon learn to quickly find the paddle and grab one end of the kayak, keeping all their things together. An instructor stands in the water helping and offering tips like "Don't think too much." These dumpings become progressively more sophisticated over the weekend until Sunday, when almost all visitors have learned how to do the classic Eskimo roll.

Instructors are enthusiastic, largely because they don't stay long enough at the camp for things to become routine. All are advanced paddlers who usually have other occupations but choose to work as instructors simply because they love being on the river.

## Madawaska Kanu Centre

Once off the river, visitors find accommodation that is functional but comfortable. A 4-hectare (10-acre) riverside campground boasts such amenities as hot showers and a sauna. There are dormitory-style cabins for those who prefer to sleep indoors, but the group is usually small enough that couples can be accommodated in their own rooms. Guests bring their own sleeping bags and pillows. A Swiss-style cedar chalet is the centre of the social activities, with a large, open fireplace. Meals are hearty European affairs, typically schnitzel, lentil soups, spinach and romaine salad and homemade European cheesecake.

Lunches are eaten on the open patio so that no one has to bother changing out of their paddling gear. After a hearty buffet of burgers, homemade soup or pita sandwiches, everyone heads back to the river to practice basic strokes, peeling into a current and eddying out, which means looking for calm pools on the side of the river where one can take a break from the rapids. Evenings are instructive: talks on technique, more paddling movies. People who are preparing for a big canoe trip will likely find something in the centre's video library about their destination, be it the Nahanni or the Coppermine.

The Madawaska Kanu Centre uses a 5-km (3-mile) section of the Madawaska River offering a range of rapids from Class 1 (barely moving) to Class 4 (only for skilled paddlers). Water is released daily from an Ontario Hydro dam upriver, ensuring fast-flowing rapids even in the middle of summer, when most rivers are low.

This section of the river is a wilderness untouched by roads or houses. Maples, oak, birch and cedar line the shore. Wildlife is abundant; typically blue herons, beavers, otters, and mink can be seen in the water or along the shoreline. For further riverside explorations visitors can walk a 3-km (2-mile) path alongside the rapids. Most folks are too tired for this in the evening, but in the early-morning hours some visitors wander this path in search of a good fishing spot where they can cast for rock bass or perch.

## if you go

**DIRECTIONS:** The Madawaska Kanu Centre is situated on the Madawaska River, near Barry's Bay, south of Algonquin Park. From Highway 60 turn south at Barry's Bay onto Dunn St. Drive south 11 km (7 miles) and turn east on Kamaniskeg Lake Rd.

**SCHEDULE:** Kayak weekends are offered from mid-May through September.

**COST:** The kayak weekends cost $174 if you camp and cook your own meals, $210 if you camp but eat the meals provided at the chalet, $244 if you stay at the indoor accommodation and eat meals at the chalet. An additional $48 rental fee covers most equipment (kayak, helmet, spray skirt, paddle). In May and June it may be necessary to add $10 for a wetsuit rental. Guests should bring sleeping bags, polypropylene underwear and a paddle jacket.

**INFORMATION:** Call (613) 594-KANU or the Toronto office at (416) 447-8845, 2 Tuna Court, Don Mills, M3A 3L1.

**MAP REFERENCE:** 1

## *Elora Gorge, Elora*

Carved by the meltwaters of retreating glaciers, this 21-m (70-foot)-deep gorge is a dramatic sight, especially with the dark Grand River surging across its floor. Hiking trails lead along both sides of the gorge, and visitors can safely peer over fenced lookouts to see the cedars and ferns that grow out of the vertical limestone walls where water seeps through the layers of rock. Caves have been carved into the soft limestone through centuries of fast-flowing water, and at Hole-in-the-Rock Lookout visitors can descend into a stony cavern. Local Natives believed that spirits inhabited the gorge.

Hiking east along the gorge, you come to the ruins of a stone granary, where the wind whistles through the empty skeleton of the building and a former cellar is overgrown with weeds. On a summer day it can be a verdant sight, but in the gray of November it is striking. The only other colour comes from a cluster of scarlet mountain ash berries and a few apples clinging to a gnarled tree grown wild.

By contrast, the town of Elora is endlessly quaint and cheerful. Long a favourite with weekend tourists who prowl through its gift and craft shops, Elora boasts many renovated historic buildings along its attractive riverside Mill St.

A charming bed-and-breakfast is The Gingerbread House, a handsome 1835 house built by the Crown's land agent and boasting such grand architectural flourishes as a 2-m (6-foot)-wide staircase. Now it is elegantly furnished with antiques and Oriental carpets. There are four guest bedrooms, where dressing gowns and slippers are provided for the walk to the bathroom down the hall. Breakfasts are served on fine china and linen, featuring specialties such as German pancakes served with spiced apples. On Sunday mornings, host Petra Veveris likes to round up her guests for her personally guided tour into the gorge.

Elora has many handsome stone buildings remaining from the days of flour power, including The Elora Mill, a grist mill until 1974 and now renovated into a popular country inn. The mill once harnessed the river to grind flour and now uses the water to generate electricity for the inn.

The attractive guest rooms are furnished with pine reproductions of antiques. A dining room and lounge both overlook the river.

Chronic shoppers can easily indulge their consumer addiction at the many boutiques and crafts shops in town. A few favourites include Naomi's, The Doll House and Holly's Secret Garden. Even the liquor store is situated in a quaint old stone building.

Elora's streets have some attractive limestone architecture, and it is well worth spending an hour or so just strolling through some of the residential neighborhoods. On Henderson St., look for St. John's Anglican Church, which has a little-known connection to Florence Nightingale. One of its early pastors, Rev. John Smithurst, was her lover and her first cousin — a fact that precluded marriage. Vowing a life of

---

*if you go*

DIRECTIONS: The Elora Gorge Conservation Area is just south of the village of Elora, 20 km (12 miles) north of Guelph. From Highway 401 head north on Highway 6 and turn west on the Elora Road (Regional Road 7). At Bloomingdale turn west and follow the signs into town.

SCHEDULE: The conservation area is open from the begining of trout season (usually early May) to Thanksgiving weekend. During winter months it is open for skiing as long as snow lasts.

ADMISSION: From opening day to Thanksgiving weekend: adults $2.75, seniors and students $2.25, children $1.75. During ski season: adults $3.25, seniors and students $2.75, children $2.25. Preschoolers free.

INFORMATION: Call the Grand River Conservation Authority, (519) 621-2761.

ACCOMMODATION/DINING: Rates at The Elora Mill range from $90 to $200 double including continental breakfast. For information contact The Elora Mill, 77 Mill St. W., Elora, N0B 1S0, (519) 846-5356. Visa, MasterCard, Amex. Rates at The Gingerbread House are $70 a couple, including breakfast. For information contact The Gingerbread House, 22 Metcalfe St. S., N0B 1S0, (519) 846-0521. Visa, MasterCard.

MAP REFERENCE: 17

## Elora Gorge

celibacy, the couple parted, with Florence going to tend the wounded in the Crimean War while Rev. Smithurst came to Elora.

The surrounding countryside offers many interesting opportunities for exploring. Head east on Road 18 and you can visit the Fergus farmers' market (see page 188), or go south on Road 21 to West Montrose for a drive through the province's only covered bridge.

*history alive*

# Crawford Lake Indian Village and Conservation Area, Milton

A meticulously reconstructed Native village, scenic Niagara Escarpment views and a rare meromictic lake combine to make Crawford Lake, near Campbellville, one of Ontario's most outstanding conservation areas.

If Crawford Lake were nothing more than a pretty place to hike in summer and cross-country ski in winter — which it is — it would still be well worth a visit. But its archeological and geological significance makes the 219-hectare (519-acre) conservation area a truly outstanding park.

Both the archeology and geology are intertwined in the development of the park, which was discovered in the early 1970s to be the site of a rare meromictic lake. These lakes are unusually deep in proportion to their small surface areas, thereby limiting the circulation of the water and depriving lower levels of oxygen. As a result, sediment collects at the lake's bottom in layers called varves. These layers can be read in much the same way as tree rings.

By analyzing the varves, scientists were able to learn about changing plant and animal life. A concentration of corn pollen between the 1434 and 1459 layers suggested agriculture associated with a Woodland Indian settlement, since corn does not grow in the wild. That, combined with finds of prehistoric tools by a local farmer, led to an archeological dig in the early 1970s, revealing a village of eleven longhouses, though perhaps not all of them existed at the same time.

The village is now reconstructed to show what it was like when partially constructed and farming was just getting under way. Inside the completed longhouse (a second longhouse is scheduled for full restoration in 1992 pending funding), the air is thick with the scent of dried corn, which was one of the dietary staples for the Iroquoian people who lived here. The staff have done a fine job of depicting Woodland Indian life by arranging a few props as though they had recently been used: corn-husk dolls, baskets made of vines and strips of wood as well as wooden farming tools. Bunches of dried plants hang from the supporting poles, with leather tags that describe their uses: thistles to cure coughs and arthritic pain, Queen Anne's lace with roots to be cooked and eaten like carrots.

The longhouse has been built based on information gathered at the time of the dig and supplemented by rudimentary drawings done by early European visitors to other sites. A sophisticated system of trusses holds up a shell of elm bark that is roughly 8 m (25 feet) high and wide. No doubt the great height helped smoke to clear from the living area.

Sleeping platforms lined with cedar boughs and furs are built along the walls. The higher platforms would have been used for storing stockpiles of corn, canoes and pottery. Lower levels were beds, though during winter months the inhabitants probably slept on the dirt floor near the fire.

A clan of roughly ninety people probably lived in this massive structure, each family group keeping its own area. Clans were matrilineal, so when a man married he moved into his wife's longhouse.

A few modern-day liberties had to be taken with the construction. To ensure safety, a layer of plywood has unobtrusively been inserted between the interior and exterior layers of bark in the walls and roof. The palisade that surrounds the village provides protection from modern-day intruders; it was not an original structure.

Visitors who want to learn more about Native life and the ecology of the area can take part in the Sunday-afternoon programs that change throughout the year. These programs may include making maple sugar in the spring, simulated archeology digs where visitors work in a grid system to uncover 500-year-old artifacts

### if you go

**DIRECTIONS:** Crawford Lake Indian Village and Conservation Area is on Steeles Ave., south of Milton. From Highway 401 exit south on the Guelph Line. Drive through Campbellville and turn east on Steeles Ave.

**SCHEDULE:** Open weekends year-round; daily during July and August from 10 a.m. to 4 p.m.

**ADMISSION:** Adults $2.50, students $2, children and seniors $1.50, preschoolers free.

**INFORMATION:** Call (416) 336-1158 or (416) 854-0234.

**MAP REFERENCE:** 11

# Crawford Lake Indian Village and Conservation Area

placed in the soil by staff, making Iroquoian pottery and learning how to make hemlock-needle tea.

The hiking trails here are lovely, varying from a quick 1.4-km (3/4-mile) jaunt around Crawford Lake to a 5.2-km (3 1/3-mile) trek through the rolling woodlands of the Pine Ridge Trail. The Bruce Trail can be reached from Crawford's network of footpaths, as it follows the Niagara Escarpment. The views are spectacular, but hikers shouldn't rush, because there are some equally lovely sights right at their feet. Wildflowers grow in abundance beginning in April with the delicate yellow trout lilies and marsh marigold, followed by violets, wild ginger, trilliums, yellow lady's slipper orchids and columbines. A free brochure that describes the area's wildflowers is available at the visitors' centre in spring. From May to October visitors may borrow all-terrain wheelchairs if required; the village and two hiking trails are wheelchair-accessible.

## Ontario Agricultural Museum, Milton

The octagonal barn has turned the head of more than one motorist zipping past Milton on Highway 401. Looming large and white, the unusual structure is now a museum piece, actually one of more than thirty historic barns, houses, workshops and other buildings that tell of our rural roots at the Ontario Agricultural Museum.

Anyone will enjoy this account of farm history, with all its hands-on experiences. Although a few displays, like methods of field drainage, have a rather limited appeal, most are geared to a wide audience and are staffed with costumed guides who gladly talk about farming and farm life in days gone by.

Live animals add a touch of realism to the farm's displays, whether it's a stray chicken pecking at some wildflowers, newborn lambs in the barn or a team of draft horses pulling a plow. Horses are often seen on weekends and special events, plowing fields, pulling farm implements and sometimes ferrying wagonloads of visitors. As a result they need regular attention. Lucky visitors might see the blacksmith firing up the forge in the 1910 blacksmith shop, ready for reshoeing. You are welcome to stand around and chat with the blacksmith as he fashions shoes appropriate to each horse's needs. Some simply require protection from wear on hard roads, and others need traction to keep steady on winter ice and spring mud. Still others need to correct posture problems with an orthopedic-type fit.

After an equine pedicure a new shoe is fitted. Red-hot from the forge, the roughly shaped shoe is held against the hoof, producing acrid smoke while the horse placidly waits. It looks painful, but the horse doesn't feel a thing because the hoof, like a human fingernail, is dead tissue.

Next door to the smithy is a harness shop, where you can learn about the next stage in readying a horse for work, the preparation of bridles, reins and other tack. The smell of leather fills the shop where well-worn horse collars and reins hang on the decorative pressed-tin walls.

Farm history isn't all horse-and-buggy stuff as visitors soon learn

*history alive*

## Ontario Agricultural Museum

when they walk through the fascinating 1928 Ford automobile and tractor dealership. The place is so authentic looking that you'd swear it was ready for customers, with its stacks of Marvelube motor oil cans and displays of Whiz tire patch. A truly offbeat antique found in this showroom is the 1913 Model-T Snowmobile. Made from a Model-T car and conversion kit, the machine was widely used by country doctors who transformed their jalopies into snow-going vehicles by adding a caterpillar rear track and front skis.

What comes as one of the most pleasant surprises is the colourful old farm machinery. I expected an unintelligible parade of gadgetry; instead I found marvelous old steam engines that are brought to life wheezing and huffing for special occasions. One of the largest agricultural equipment collections in North America, the museum holds gems like the Richardson wooden butter churn, painted bright red and stenciled with roses in a style more reminiscent of a gypsy wagon than the commercial dairy for which it was intended. Inventiveness is the hallmark of farm equipment, like the treadle-powered churn that could be powered by the family dog.

Farming is presented in a broad perspective here with displays on a wide range of subjects from cider-making to a modern milking parlour. Oddly eclectic collections are often the most interesting, like the collection of 875 wax fruits and vegetables made at the turn of the century by Elizabeth Potter as a teaching tool for the University of Guelph. It shows species of apples seldom heard of today.

From the early days of hewing log cabins out of virgin wilderness to today's often computerized farms, agriculture has seen many changes in the past century and a half. Farmsteads dispersed across the site show visitors the evolution of Ontario farm life from a crude log cabin to a slightly more developed 1830s farmstead and then the relative luxury of the 1860s clapboard house with its gingerbread veranda and fine front parlour. Gardens are planted only with varieties of seed contemporary to their period: tomatoes abound in an 1860 garden, for example, but are absent from one showing plants only thirty years earlier, when the fruit was believed poisonous.

The buildings are usually buzzing with activity, such as the spinning and weaving at the weaver's cottage, where a great cauldron hangs from an outdoor tripod, ready for a brew of natural dyes. Visitors are likely to find a costumed guide baking biscuits over the hearth in the 1830s farmhome or stitching a fine piece of needlework in the parlour of the 1860s home.

Although there is always something going on at the museum from May to September, it is best to time a visit to coincide with one of the special events held throughout the season. Canada Day celebrations on July 1 always feature an old-fashioned flag-waving party. The Great Canadian Antique Tractor Field Days in mid-July are a great opportunity to see some classic old engines wheezing and chugging. During the Family Corn Festival in late August you can munch some sweet cobs, then learn how thrifty pioneers made corn-husk dolls, brooms and mattress stuffing. A Harvest Festival and Farmers' Market is held in mid-September.

---

*if you go*

**DIRECTIONS:** The Ontario Agricultural Museum is on Tremaine Rd., west of Milton. Take either Exit 312 or 320 from Highway 401 and follow the signs.

**SCHEDULE:** Open daily from early May to mid-September from 10 a.m. to 5 p.m.

**ADMISSION:** Adults $3.50, seniors and youths $1.75, family $8.50, children 5 and under free.

**INFORMATION:** Call (416) 878-8151

**MAP REFERENCE:** 11

---

*history alive*

## Petroglyphs Provincial Park, Bancroft

Carved into Canadian Shield granite, the depictions of men, animals and mystic images in Petroglyphs Provincial Park are said to be the largest concentration of prehistoric rock carvings in Canada.

Although estimated to be 500 to 1,000 years old, the petroglyphs became widely known only during the 1950s, when geologists searching for mineral deposits stumbled upon them. Since then, the precious carvings have been exposed to the destructive effects of the numerous visitors who have not hesitated to add their own "Kilroy Was Here" carvings.

Now these priceless pictures are protected in an airy glass shelter that lets visitors see the glyphs in natural sunlight while keeping out the rain, wind and snow that would wear the edges of the carvings. Controlled heat prevents winter shattering of the rock: controlled humidity also helps curtail the spread of algae, which darken the rock's white surface, obscuring the carvings. A well-designed viewing area allows visitors to see the carvings from different levels. To increase their visibility, the carvings have been coloured with black grease pencil.

An informed staff — typically anthropology students — explains the significance of the rock carvings, believed to be carved by the Algonkians. As many as 900 carvings have been found on the site, 300 of which can be interpreted. Since the carvings are often layered one on top of another, many have already been obscured.

Spread over an area 14 m by 24 m (45 by 80 feet), the petroglyphs don't tell any story, but they do have mythological and religious significance. A typical recurring theme is the turtle, surrounded by dots, which has become the park's own symbol. Many tribes believe that the world was built on a turtle's back. The dots represent eggs, which are also the symbol of fertility.

The natural world was full of mythological meaning for the Algonkians, who drew on this inspiration in the themes for the carvings. The salamander that sheds its skin becomes a symbol of life renewal, and a long-legged crane could serve as both a clan symbol and a symbol of the freedom and immortality of the soul. Both can be found among the carvings.

Unusual landscape formations are said to have held a special appeal for the shamans who likely carved the rocks while in a trance. White rock may have been a symbol of purity, and the cracks and fissures that split its surface all add to its spiritual significance. A vein of iron oxide is worked into the image of a woman straddling the red stream, thought to be a depiction of menstruation.

The shamans themselves are represented, often with projections engraved around their heads, almost like cartoon conversation bubbles. These projections and distortions are said to represent the shaman's dreamlike state as he worked on the carvings with a hammerstone, like the piece of gneiss that visitors are shown, one of more than thirty such stones found on the site.

Boats are represented repeatedly on the rock, but they are not engraved as familiar canoes but as strange vessels with rudders and perhaps even sails. These are believed to be mystic solar boats, permitting magical travel through the universe to look for lost souls.

Provincial park staff have become increasingly sensitive to Native concerns in recent years, and now members of the nearby Curve Lake Reserve have access to this important site for private traditional ceremonies.

In addition to the petroglyphs, the park has two attractive woodland hiking trails: High Falls (10 km/6 miles) and Nanabush (4 km/2 1/2 miles).

*if you go*

DIRECTIONS: Petroglyphs Provincial Park is halfway between Peterborough and Bancroft. From Peterborough drive 44 km (27 miles) north on Highway 28 to Northey's Bay Rd. Look for the park sign and drive 11 km (7 miles) east.

SCHEDULE: Open mid-May to Thanksgiving daily 10 a.m. to 5 p.m., July and August 10 a.m. to 6 p.m.

ADMISSION: $5.75 per vehicle. Ontario seniors free.

INFORMATION: May through October (705) 877-2552. At other times contact the Ministry of Natural Resources in Bancroft at (613) 332-3940.

MAP REFERENCE: 4

## Lang Pioneer Village, Peterborough

Situated beside a millpond, along the grassy banks of the Indian River, Lang Pioneer Village enjoys an idyllic site where it is easy to forget the twentieth century and fall into the slower pace of nineteenth-century life. Depicting the daily round of pioneer life, the village reflects the pace of the seasons: sheep-shearing in the spring, corn roasts in August, an apple festival in the fall and dog-sledding in winter. Visitors can attend a mini history lesson at the modern visitors' centre, then stroll through the collection of two dozen historic homes and businesses.

The Lang Grist Mill is occasionally pressed into service grinding whole-wheat flour (sold at the gift shop). Flour has a special significance for this village, since it is the site of David Fife's 1820s log cabin. Fife, who at the age of fifteen emigrated from Scotland to Canada, was one of the first farmers who realized that the European strains of wheat were not suited to the Canadian climate. He wrote to a friend back home for new seed samples and began a horticultural experiment that led to the development of Red Fife wheat, one of the hardy strains that opened up the Canadian West to agriculture.

Fife lived in this one-room cabin with his wife and three children. Though it seems cosy at first glimpse, a closer look shows life pared down to its barest necessities — a box bed that could be folded into a bench during the day, and an all-purpose stone hearth for winter warmth and cooking. Outdoors, a costumed guide can often be found heating a cauldron full of wax over an open fire, getting ready for candle-making.

Prosperous settlers may have gone on to build an improved second home like the 1848 Fitzpatrick House, which seems positively roomy with its 2-m (6 1/2-foot)-wide stone fireplace. Its gardens are planted with herbs and vegetables, lending it a lived-in look. In fact, the entire village succeeds in creating that impression. Laundry hangs on a line outdoors. Goats and pigs are kept in simple pens behind split-rail fences. A rooster ambles about a yard, pecking at the ground.

One of the latest period houses is the Milbrun log house, restored to the 1870s when a newlywed couple bought it along with a farm. Indoors it has such luxuries as a kitchen sink with a pump to draw water from a cistern, as well as a lovely cast-iron stove, which is still used whenever one of the costumed guides bakes cookies or scones.

More than just displaying the homes of the pioneers, the village also shows their skills and crafts. In the Hastie Carpenter Shop a carpenter working with nineteenth-century tools makes rolling pins, chairs and wooden toys. Long curls of shaved wood are often fascinating enough toys for the young children who watch him plane a plank. Every Sunday the blacksmith shop, an 1880 print shop and the shingle mill are in action. There is even an old tinsmithing shop where pitchers, mugs, candelabra and apple corers are made.

Modern-day travelers always seem to be amused by the 1870s Keene Hotel, once a family-run stagecoach stop on the Hastings-Peterborough road. Seven children lived in the house, along with the coming and going guests. Their toys, including a tin train, can be seen strewn about the parlour. Rates posted at the front office seem like a bargain — 75 cents for the best room and 10 cents a flop — until visitors go upstairs to inspect the rooms. The best room is fine enough: a crocheted quilt covers the double bed and a round tin bathtub represents the most modern convenience. But the flop is just that, a burlap bag stuffed with straw lying on the floor, eight flops to a room. A black cat sleeping on the

### if you go

**DIRECTIONS:** Lang Pioneer Village is southeast of Peterborough. From Highway 7 turn south on County Road 34 (Heritage Line). Watch for the sign; if your reach the village of Keene, you have gone too far.

**SCHEDULE:** The visitors' centre is open daily May 10 to October 20, same hours as the village; rest of the year, daily 1 to 5 p.m. The village is open daily from mid-May to late October, weekdays 11 a.m. to 5 p.m., Saturdays 1 to 5 p.m., Sundays 1 to 6 p.m. Special occasions are held year-round (see above for examples).

**ADMISSION:** Adults $5, seniors and students $4, children $2.50, children under 5 free

**INFORMATION:** Call (705) 295-6694

**MAP REFERENCE:** 4

*history alive* 47

## Lang Pioneer Village

straw sack was probably a good indicator that this accommodation was not guaranteed to be flea-free.

The 1858 Menie General Store and Post Office has been restored to its 1890s appearance, the shelves now stocked with old tea tins, tonics such as May Apple Bitters, and laundry aids such as Rickitts Blue.

Children find the old South Lake School particularly instructive. There, a teacher invites them to sit down at one of the double desks and learn how to write on a slate. The one-room school is outfitted with such Victorian teaching aids as the 1890s charts that provide pictorial lessons in a school where they likely couldn't afford a book for each child.

Many special events are held throughout the year at Lang. Sheep-shearing is done on the Sunday of the Victoria Day long weekend. One Sunday in mid July is declared Flour Mill Day, with horse-and-wagon rides and milling demonstrations. The Otonabee Pioneer Contests Day held on the Sunday of the August Civic Holiday weekend features a giant corn roast. Pioneer Craft Day on Labour Day Sunday is a celebration of old-time skills, with roughly forty craftspeople demonstrating skills from straw-hat braiding to honey-separating. In December Lang's Victorian Christmas Festival offers romantic sleigh rides, snowshoeing, a giant bonfire, a visit from Father Christmas and lessons in making decorations. Winter Festivals are great days outdoors with sleigh rides, snowshoes and snowmen, followed by warming cider at the visitors' centre. Food plays a big part in most celebrations here.

# Fort George National Historic Park, Niagara-on-the-Lake

While theatrical productions lure droves of summer visitors to Niagara-on-the-Lake's Shaw Festival, another drama just down the road from the theatre is well worth catching. During summer months costumed staff enact the roles of soldiers, wives and other personnel who would have been stationed at Fort George on the eve of the War of 1812.

From the outside, this log fortress looks decidedly unimposing, but it was the scene of a dramatic battle that saw the British come close to losing much of their North American colony. Today, as visitors walk the shady tree-lined paths listening to the shrieks of cheeky blue jays, it takes some imagination to picture this pretty tourist town under American attack.

From a grassy slope you can see the rival Fort Niagara on the American side of the Niagara River, almost within spitting distance. Built by the French and then won by the British, Fort Niagara was finally surrendered to the Americans in 1796, thereby requiring Britain to build the much newer Fort George on the Canadian (or British) side of the river.

In heated border battles, Fort George was burned to the ground and abandoned to the Americans in May of 1813. More than a century later it was reconstructed as a make-work project during the Great Depression. Research was hurried, but the craftsmanship was done with attention to historic detail. Wood was cut by hand in a saw pit and nails pounded in a forge.

What often surprises visitors as they cross the dry moat and enter the fort is the size of the place. It seems more like a farm within a stockade than an actual fort. These roomy proportions reflect peacetime living, with space for gardens, games and numerous tents. During the war it was scaled down to facilitate defense.

Like visitors in 1812, you will probably stop first at the guardhouse, where a shelf bed allowed soldiers (fully dressed, right down to their buttoned gaiters) a few hours' rest between watches. Prisoners were kept here in windowless cells, aptly referred to as black holes, which they shared with rodents. Outside stands an easellike structure known

*history alive* **49**

## Fort George National Historic Park

as the punishment triangle, where offenders were whipped with a cat-o'-ninetails. Whippings sound severe to us, but the nineteenth-century soldier was not the epitome of the fighting stalwart. According to one 1840s British survey, only two out of 120 men in a typical unit could be described as respectable persons induced into military life after falling upon misfortune. The rest were discovered to be idlers, criminals, bad characters and black sheep in need of discipline.

At times, though, discipline became too severe, and in 1803 mutiny was afoot. General Brock came from York to investigate and saw seven men executed. After that episode he greatly relaxed the rigid atmosphere at Fort George and allowed men vegetable gardens, soccer-style sports and game hunting — providing they paid for their own ammunition.

If the fort resembles a farmstead, then the officers' quarters might be described as the farmhouse. A yellow-painted clapboard house surrounded by a white picket fence reveals a lifestyle suited to a gentleman. In the sitting room a woman often plays period tunes on the pianoforte, and a punch bowl is set out with a silver ladle, as though for a soirée. An officer, dressed for the 41st Regiment, greets visitors and points out some of the niceties a junior officer might have enjoyed, like netting around his canopied bed to ward off malarial mosquitoes, then a serious problem in this part of Ontario.

Life in the blockhouse was a very different story. Here enlisted men slept fifty to a room. Out of every hundred soldiers, six were allowed wives and slept in "married quarters," which meant only that they hung a blanket around the bunk for privacy. Children slept wherever they could find a space.

Self-sufficiency was crucial in the New World. Craftsmen known as artificers maintained and manufactured assorted oddments from hinges to handles, nails to gun fittings. In the artificer's shop a visitor typically finds a blacksmith busy making nails to be used in repairs and restoration.

Anyone looking for a touch of history in the accommodations, or just plain good value while staying in the Niagara area, should try the

Niagara-on-the-Lake Bed and Breakfast service run by Luciana Siciliano. She will find you accommodation as well as make reservations for dinner and theatre. Visitors' tastes are matched with an appropriate host, with properties ranging from a grand Victorian house to simpler country homes.

## if you go

**DIRECTIONS:** Fort George National Historic Park is on the Niagara Parkway in Niagara-on-the-Lake. From the Queen Elizabeth Way take Highway 55 north through Virgil to Niagara-on-the-Lake and follow the Canadian Parks Service beaver signs.

**SCHEDULE:** Open daily from the Victoria Day weekend to the end of October. May and June 9 a.m. to 5 p.m., July to Labour Day 10 a.m. to 6 p.m., September and October 10 a.m. to 5 p.m.

**ADMISSION:** Adults $2.25, seniors $1.50, children and students $1, children under 6 free, family $5.50.

**INFORMATION:** Call (416) 468-4257

**ACCOMMODATION:** The Niagara-on-the-Lake Bed and Breakfast Service prices range from $55 to $110, but most are at the lower end. Contact Niagara-on-the-Lake Bed and Breakfast, Box 1515, Niagara-on-the-Lake, L0S 1J0, telephone (416) 358-8988.

**MAP REFERENCE:** 13

## Battlefield House, Stoney Creek

L ooking out over the expanse of parkland that surrounds Battlefield House, you would never guess that it was the scene of one of the most dramatic battles in Canadian history.

By June 6, 1813, the British had nearly lost Upper Canada to the invading Americans. Their commanding officer, Maj. Gen. Sir Isaac Brock, was killed. York was burned and so was the government supply depot at Burlington Beach. Fort George, too, had been torched, forcing the British to retreat from the Niagara area while roughly 3,000 American soldiers advanced across the Niagara Peninsula as far as Stoney Creek.

At Burlington Heights the British would make their last stand. U.S. troops followed in hot pursuit from Niagara to Stoney Creek, a small community near Burlington Heights that was strategically situated on crossroads. The invading Americans commandered a farmhouse belonging to James Gage as their headquarters, confining the Gage family (grandmother, mother and five children) to the cellar. James Gage had already been captured while working in the fields.

Although we often think of nineteenth-century warfare as tidy rows of foot soldiers firing well-timed volleys into each other's ranks, this battle was won with a surprise manoeuvre — an essential move since the British were outnumbered by more than four to one. During a night attack, U.S. guards were captured. In heavy fighting, twenty British soldiers rushed the U.S. guns and were able to take four of the six. The U.S. cavalry was pushed back, running into their own men, and U.S. troops scattered.

Fearing their small numbers would be discovered, the British retreated to Burlington. The Americans, after briefly returning to destroy equipment, withdrew to Forty Mile Creek, where they were fired upon by the navy, local militia and Indians, forcing them back to Fort George. Having sorely weakened the Americans' morale, the small British detachment at Stoney Creek had profoundly affected the outcome of the war.

The Gages' house lasted through the battle; it weathered a few musket wounds but was otherwise unharmed. James Gage survived the war to become a prosperous businessman with various dockside enterprises in Burlington Heights that enabled him to enlarge the house to an elegant two stories.

Today Battlefield House and the grounds are open to the public. Costumed guides explain life as the Gages would probably have lived it as they lead visitors through the rooms.

Remarkably, some of the original decor in this pretty frame house has survived a century and a half of renovation, decay and restoration. Now protected by a sheet of Plexiglas, a section of the front hallway shows the original decorative stenciling on the plaster walls. The hunter green and cherry red patterns are still vivid, a testimony to the quality of early paints. Careful restoration has been done in the house now filled with period furniture and even a few items originally belonging to the Gages.

Visitors often arrive to find a spicy aroma emanating from the keeping-room hearth where the day's baking is under way. A freshly baked treat is often ready to be sampled, typically a scone, oatcake or piece of dark spice cake to munch while a costumed guide talks about the kitchen gadgets of old.

Visitors of all ages enjoy a chance to try out some of the nineteenth-century equipment in the pantry as they are invited to grind coffee beans by hand or pinch pieces of sugar off the hard cone with sugar snips. From the larder window you can look out over the manicured lawn where soldiers once scrambled in the night raid.

A roomy parlour with plenty of

*if you go*

DIRECTIONS: Battlefield House is at 77 King St. W., in Stoney Creek. Take the Highway 20 exit (Centennial Parkway) south from the Queen Elizabeth Way and turn left at King St.

SCHEDULE: Open Victoria Day weekend through Thanksgiving, Sunday to Friday 1 to 4 p.m. During July and August, daily 11 a.m. to 5 p.m. Open at other times for special events.

ADMISSION: Adults $1.25, seniors $1, children 60 cents.

INFORMATION: Call (416) 662-8458

MAP REFERENCE: 12

## Battlefield House

space for entertaining reflects the Gage family's prominent social standing. A table is set with fine china, as though visitors were expected for tea. The original key still opens the door to the cellar where the Gage family sat out the battle. In those days, though, the cellar floor was mud, not concrete. Children enjoy having the lights turned out and imagining the melee outside while the family waited in the dark to discover the outcome.

A second-floor museum displays artifacts from the battle: rusty bayonets and buttons, cannon balls and bar shot. Each year on the first weekend of June the anniversary of the Battle of Stoney Creek is commemorated with a spectacular military encampment. Usually well over a dozen reenactment groups, including the local Lincoln Militia, turn out for a weekend of costumed drills and battles.

Visitors are invited to tour the encampment to see how soldiers and their followers lived. Camp women often served as nurses. Artisans demonstrate their crafts, and period music is performed.

Another great time to visit Battlefield House is December, when candlelight evenings are offered on three special evenings.

# The Hamilton Museum of Steam and Technology, Hamilton

The Hamilton Museum of Steam and Technology is the kind of museum that should change Canadians' perception of the past. While numerous pioneer museums tell the story of the Loyalists and immigrant settlers who scraped a living out of the backwoods, the Hamilton Museum of Steam and Technology shows that Canada was not only a nation of hewers of wood and drawers of water but a place of industrial and technological development.

One of the major accomplishments in urban technology was the pumping of clean water to homes and industries. Hamilton was a pioneer in this respect by having a pumping station as early as 1859 complete with massive engines and flywheels built at local foundries, an impressive feat for the young colony. The attractive architecture of the stone building that houses the machinery reflects the pride that must have been felt for this ambitious public works project.

Today the pump house is a museum, with the original Gartshore Beam Engines lovingly restored. Visitors enter the pump house for a close-up look at the 7-m (24-foot) flywheels and 15-tonne beams, in mansionlike surroundings of ornate Grecian columns, gleaming brass and polished woodwork. Although they had been operational until recently, the engines now require restorative work that will be done when funding is available. To see them in motion, visitors are invited to turn the massive flywheels by hand.

Built through a combination of foresight and necessity, the pump house radically altered the direction of Hamilton's development. During the 1840s Hamilton's 10,000-strong population was quickly growing as shiploads of new immigrants arrived after long ocean voyages. With them they brought the shipboard disease cholera, which quickly contaminated wells and reached epidemic proportions during hot summer months.

A steady supply of clean pumped water would not only prevent the cholera from spreading but it would also help Hamilton compete in attracting manufacturing and textile industries, which were often lured

*history alive*

## *The Hamilton Museum of Steam and Technology*

by neighboring Dundas with its natural water supply.

Housed in a noble building of sandstone and limestone, the massive engines embody the glory of Victorian industrial engineering; civic pride was at stake then, and city fathers came close to sparing no expense. The cast-iron engine cylinders are encased in mahogany panels and gleaming brass rings, looking fit for a royal inspection.

The total cost of the 1859 pumping station was $600,000, and this deserves to be noted in Canada's history as an example of a public works project that was built on schedule and on budget.

A gallery in the old boiler room displays changing exhibits related to technology, often with engineering models and a collection of historical photos of the construction of the pump house.

---

*if you go*

**DIRECTIONS:** The Hamilton Museum of Steam and Technology is at 900 Woodward Ave. in Hamilton. From the Queen Elizabeth Way westbound take Centennial Parkway South. Turn right at Barton St. E., and then right at Woodward Ave.

**SCHEDULE:** Open daily year-round. June 1 to August 31, 11 a.m. to 4 p.m. September through May, noon to 4 p.m.

**ADMISSION:** Adults $2, seniors and students $1.50, children $1.25, children under 5 free.

**INFORMATION:** Call (416) 549-5225

**MAP REFERENCE:** 12

## Sainte-Marie Among the Hurons, Midland

One of history's most bizarre juxtapositions has to be seventeenth-century French Jesuits in the remote forests of Huronia. From the European cathedral to the smoke-filled aboriginal longhouses, the cultural gap was immense. Today, visitors can explore this cultural difference at Sainte-Marie Among the Hurons, a reconstruction of the seventeenth-century Jesuit community of priests and Huron converts in the wilderness near what today is the town of Midland.

Visitors are given a succinct history of the site at a visitors' centre where a museum relates the site to developments in Europe and Canada at that time, using a wide range of artifacts such as seventeenth-century tools, a seventeenth-century papal bull relating to the neighboring Martyrs' Shrine, built in 1926, and a display of Native canoe-building. Afterward a slick film presentation dramatizes the confrontations between Huron traditionalists and Christian missionaries. Visiting Sainte-Marie is like being part of a large drama, so when the film ends and the screen becomes a door opening out onto the site, visitors have the feeling that they are stepping into the action.

This ongoing production is set in a cluster of rudely crafted wooden buildings within Sainte-Marie's palisade and is acted out by characters — usually university students in costume — such as a missionary or Huron convert. The characters converse directly with visitors as well as take part in staged dramas like the arrival of a canoe flotilla bearing supplies from distant Quebec, or an account of Iroquois attacks on distant villages. Continuing research benefits the development of these characters.

Once inside the stockade, you will easily believe you have been transported back to 1640s Huronia. All the sights and smells are perfect: wooden timbers for the reconstructed buildings have been roughly hewn with an adze, chickens scratch and peck in an animal compound and the jobs of baking bread, repairing tools and organizing stores goes on just as it would have 350 years ago. Only the sounds of English being spoken give away its modern-day museum status.

You can walk freely through the site, stopping to ask questions of

## Sainte-Marie Among the Hurons

costumed interpreters. At the spartan church or the missionaries' quarters you might hear Father Paul Ragueneau talking about his Christian mission to bring salvation to the New World. Wandering through the Native quarters where Hurons are tanning hides and weaving baskets in the longhouse compound, you might hear a different story: a Native woman, Yawainoh, laments that her family is dying from disease and that foreign ideas are creating social tension and breaking up families.

When the reconstructed site opened in 1967 it emphasized the missionary life, but in recent years much has been done to address that imbalance by developing the Native area of the compound. Now visitors get a thorough look at life in the longhouse, the communal building that was home to the Hurons. Among the smoke-filled shadows are the trappings of Huron life: the furs and dried corn and tobacco. A woman is cooking a meal in the traditional way, using hot stones to heat cornmeal in a clay pot that could not withstand the direct heat of the fire.

When Christian missionaries introduced useful new technology, including copper pots, iron fish hooks and axes, woolen blankets and cool, cotton chemises, their ideas about God were made quite palatable. The attendant benefits of new tools made it easy to understand why such Hurons as the newly christened Jean-Baptiste were eager to embrace Catholicism.

The cultural exchange was a two-way affair, however, and visitors see how the Jesuits adopted many Huron

---

### *if you go*

**DIRECTIONS:** Sainte-Marie Among the Hurons is on Highway 12 just east of Midland, directly opposite the Martyrs' Shrine. From Highway 400 exit west on Highway 12.

**SCHEDULE:** Open Victoria Day weekend through Thanksgiving, daily 10 a.m. to 5 p.m.

**ADMISSION:** Adults $5.75, youths $3.50, seniors $3.25, children under 6 free. Admission slightly reduced after Labour Day. Candlelight Tours cost $5.50 for adults, $3.50 for children, and must be booked in advance.

**INFORMATION:** Call (705) 526-7838

**MAP REFERENCE:** 9

habits, particularly when it came to food. A granary is stocked with such typical Huron produce as dried corn.

The cultural cross-fertilization is also reflected in the special events held throughout the year at the site, ranging from programs of seventeenth-century French song to Native drama. Try a candlelight tour as an unusual way to see the site.

## *The Meeting Place, St. Jacobs*

A blinkered horse waits patiently in front of the smithy while its driver talks to the blacksmith about new buggy wheels and perhaps a harness. It's a scene that belongs to nineteenth-century Ontario, but here in St. Jacobs it's just part of another typical working day. This is Mennonite country, where many members of the religion's Old Order shun technology and cling to the old traditions: horse and buggy, dark clothes and muslin caps.

In fact, only a minority of Ontario's Mennonites fit this description; many others adapt to modern life quite easily. But it is the quaint picture of the Old Order Mennonites in their horse-drawn buggies that entices so many visitors to this area.

The Mennonite way of life and beliefs are explained at the Meeting Place, a St. Jacobs museum run by Mennonites. Although the Old Order ways that draw so much attention are simple, the Meeting Place offers a sophisticated multimedia presentation employing film, audio and slide shows as well as photo collections and some museum displays.

An interesting twenty-eight-minute film, *Mennonites of Ontario*, introduces visitors to the basic beliefs in the "seven-days-a-week" religion whose members embrace the principle of brotherly love in a practical way by offering neighbors a helping hand, whether clearing debris after a storm or working together at a barn-raising.

Assessing the spiritual costs of technological advancement is a recurring theme in the film, which illustrates how Old Order Mennonites have preferred "to preserve the plain way" in the hope that it will reinforce traditional family values. It is an irony that the simple style the Old Order has embraced to maintain its humility has drawn the attention of so many visitors, many of whom are appallingly insensitive in the way they snap shots of people in buggies as though they were just costumed characters at a tourist attraction.

The most effective of the Meeting Place's displays is a reconstruction of an old-fashioned country kitchen that tells as much about Old Order life as any wordy bit of signage. The simple wooden table is set for an ordinary meal that will become a family get-together. Bottles of preserves and a butter churn are signs of the plain, hardworking life.

Mennonite craftsmanship and the area's growing appeal for tourists have prompted a mushrooming of craft and antique shops, most of which stay open seven days a week to take advantage of the busy weekend traffic. A walk down King St., which has many craft and specialty shops, may leave visitors with the impression that quilting is the cornerstone of the local economy. Quilted pillows, placemats, tablecloths, teapot covers and bedspreads are all displayed in abundance in shop windows. Many of the bedspreads are locally made by Mennonite women who use traditional patterns such as the fan or lone star.

Jakobstettel Guest House is the perfect base for exploring the area's excellent markets and craft and quilt shops. A turn-of-the-century mansion that has been carefully restored, it has an old atmosphere that fits perfectly with the spirit of St. Jacobs. The Victorian red-brick house was built in 1898 by William Snider and restored during the early 1980s by a local consortium. Twelve guest rooms, each with a bathroom, are named after local notables and are furnished with antique and reproduction pieces in keeping with Jakobstettel's Victorian character.

Sitting on 2 hectares (5 acres) of grounds, it is a quiet spot for unwinding. The banks of the mill race provide a pretty setting for a walk or cross-country skiing. During the summer an outdoor pool and tennis court are available. Guests can borrow bicycles to explore the area in a mode of transport that seems in keeping with the character of the village.

Benjamin's Restaurant and Inn is the oldest building in town, built in 1852. After a sorry decline into beer parlour, the inn was resurrected in the 1980s, completely renovated and refurbished. Attractive white stucco dining rooms have prominent fireplaces, and the food is usually well prepared. Guest bedrooms provide modern conveniences like colour TV and air-conditioning but still manage to look folksy.

It is worth getting up early on Saturday to catch the famous farmers'

*history alive*

## The Meeting Place

market in nearby Waterloo. Ever since Kitchener dressed up its market to look like a shopping mall, the Waterloo County Farmers' Market has become popular with aficionados of old-fashioned crafts and food. Look for local specialties such as well-smoked summer sausage or cooked cheese, a smooth cheese made from skim milk. The market is on Weber St. N., half a kilometer (1/3 mile) outside Waterloo city limits. The St Jacobs Farmers' Market is just on the other side of Weber St. Come early because the action starts at 6 a.m. on Saturdays and finishes by midafternoon.

### if you go

DIRECTIONS: St. Jacobs is about 8 km (5 miles) north of Waterloo. From Waterloo take Highway 86 north to Regional Road 17 and turn west. The Meeting Place is at 33 King St.

SCHEDULE: The Meeting Place is open year-round. From May through October, weekdays 11 a.m. to 5 p.m., Saturdays 10 a.m. to 5 p.m., Sundays 1:30 to 5 p.m. From November through April, Saturdays 11 a.m. to 4:30 p.m. and Sundays 2 to 4:30 p.m.

ADMISSION: Free, but donations are appreciated.

INFORMATION: Call (519) 664-3518

ACCOMMODATION: Jakobstettel Guest House, 16 Isabella St., St. Jacobs, charges $100 to $150 double, including breakfast. For information call (519) 664-2208. Visa, MasterCard, Amex.

Benjamin's Restaurant and Inn, 17 King St., charges $90 to $100 double. For information call (519) 664-3731. Visa, MasterCard, Amex, EnRoute.

St. Jacobs Farmers' Market and Flea Market, (519) 747-1830, is at King and Weber streets, north of Waterloo, just south of St. Jacobs. The Waterloo County Farmers' Market, (519) 664-2817, is directly across Weber St. Both feature local produce and crafts.

MAP REFERENCE: 16

## heroes & houses

## *Norman Bethune Memorial House, Gravenhurst*

More than half a century has passed since Norman Bethune, the crusading surgeon, died from an infection while volunteering at the front lines during the Sino-Japanese War. Yet his memory looms larger as time passes. In recent years his flamboyant character and accomplished career have been celebrated in television documentaries and a megabuck movie, but to really understand the roots of Bethune's drive and ambition, there is no substitute for a visit to the nineteenth-century house in Gravenhurst where Bethune was born.

The Canadian Parks Service now administers Bethune Memorial House, and they have done an admirable job of chronicling the doctor's life in a second-floor display that employs old photographs, artifacts and written panels to lead visitors through a startling range of his achievements.

The display begins with a collection of antique toys (fitting the place and the period, though not actually belonging to Bethune) and anecdotes about his childhood. As the son of a Presbyterian minister and missionary mother, Bethune seemed destined to serve others. One story tells how as a child skating on a frozen lake with his friends, he saw a boy fall through the ice. While others looked on in fear and confusion, the young Bethune took action and rescued the lad.

There is a brief description, with photos, of his two stormy marriages — both to the same woman, the wealthy Frances Campbell Penny. After a spendthrift lifestyle in Detroit during the Roaring Twenties and a broken marriage, Bethune faced a bout of tuberculosis that brought him back to Gravenhurst, where he rested at the sanatorium. Ill health seems to have given him time to contemplate his life, and after successful treatment he went back to his studies in Montreal, continuing to work in thoracic surgery while developing surgical innovations. Tools he invented, like the Bethune Rib Shears displayed here, are still in use today.

While in Montreal he became concerned about the social causes of disease. Interested in socialized medicine, he ran free clinics during the

64   *heroes & houses*

Depression at the Verdun YMCA and began to advocate a public health care system.

Horrified by the rise of fascism in the Spanish Civil War, he volunteered his services. Graphic photos of wounded children help visitors understand the outrage that moved Bethune. He toiled on the front lines with his innovative mobile blood-transfusion units, but also raised funds in Canada to build a 500-bed orphanage.

While back in Canada for a speaking tour, Bethune heard of the Japanese invasion of China, and equating the Chinese struggle to Spain's, he headed for the Orient where Mao Tse-tung invited him to supervise the Eighth Route Army Border Hospital. A brief video chronicles his struggle to save lives while working in the rough conditions of a military front. Bethune's spirit of sacrifice seemed limitless: he often had to operate without gloves and gave away his personal emergency kit of drugs.

Not surprisingly, Bethune remains a hero of the Revolution fifty years later, and Chinese delegations often make pilgrimages to the Gravenhurst museum. Signs are trilingual (English, French and Chinese) to aid the approximately 700 visitors each year from the People's Republic of China.

In addition to the biographical display, visitors may tour the bedrooms and ground floor of the house, a clapboard Presbyterian manse restored, in the meticulous fashion for which the Canadian Parks Service is noted, to the year 1890 when Norman Bethune was born in a bedroom upstairs.

With all its Victorian finery, the house seems an unlikely beginning for a self-sacrificing crusader.

*if you go*

DIRECTIONS: The Norman Bethune Memorial House is in Gravenhurst, at 235 John St. From Highway 11, take the Gravenhurst exit, proceed on Bethune Dr., following the brown-and-yellow signs to the house.
SCHEDULE: Open daily year-round.
ADMISSION: Free.
INFORMATION: Call (705) 687-4261
MAP REFERENCE: 10

## Norman Bethune Memorial House

Portraits of the young Victoria and Albert hang on the parlour wall, seemingly surveying all the comforts of middle-class life: a lovely Eastlake parlour suite, an ornate pump organ (complete with patented mouse-proof pedals) and a pair of paper-mâché chairs with elaborate mother-of-pearl inlay. They are luxuries that were not unheard of in Gravenhurst's boom days, when fourteen lumber mills operated on Muskoka Bay and good train service made a trip to Toronto simpler than the present-day drive down the traffic-clogged Highway 400.

So thorough is the restoration of the house that the appropriate number and style of coats for the Bethune family hang on pegs in the front hallway. The dining-room table is set, typically with teacups and a plate of macaroons. On a parlour chair lies a cuffed, mauve shawl — "one of Mrs. Bethune's favourite colours," says the guide, as though Mrs. Bethune were about to walk in and put it on.

The details are meticulous: for much of the year the clock is one hour behind (there was no Daylight Saving Time in the 1890s), the pantry is stocked with goods of the era, including authentic cans of tomato soup, and the child's high chair is smattered with crumbs as though Baby Norman had just eaten his morning snack.

The Bethune family would have been familiar with the steamers that plied the Muskoka waters a century ago. Today visitors can ride one of those wonderful old boats, now lovingly restored. The R.M.S. *Segwun* takes passengers on afternoon and day trips during the summer months. See page 114.

## Hutchison House Museum, Peterborough

When Dr. John Hutchison immigrated to Upper Canada in 1818 he came to a Peterborough where the streets were still dotted with tree stumps and the houses were mostly log cabins. The civic-minded young doctor worked hard for the growing community; to make ends meet he spent spare hours serving as a justice of the peace and a sergeant in the local militia. But by 1826 he found it nearly impossible to make a living for himself and his large family of seven children. Moving to York (now Toronto) seemed inevitable.

Afraid of losing their beloved doctor, the citizens of Peterborough pooled their resources and labor to build an attractive stone house that would induce him to stay. A century and a half later the citizens of Peterborough once again pooled their resources to restore the doctor's house to its original condition, making it into a living history museum.

Today costumed guides show visitors around the historic home and explain the lifestyle of its earliest occupants, including the Hutchisons' famous boarder, Sandford Fleming, who had recently come to Canada and was staying with the doctor, his cousin. Some extraordinary insights into the Hutchison family's nineteenth-century life are provided by the diaries and letters of the Scottish-born Fleming, the railway construction engineer who surveyed the route of the Canadian Pacific, became chancellor of Queen's University and introduced time zones to North America.

As a doctor, Hutchison was a pillar of the growing community. His wife played an important role entertaining patients in a front parlour that doubled as a waiting room — in fact, the table is set for tea as though patients were expected at any moment.

Perhaps her most arduous task was that of setting community standards for cleanliness, no doubt a difficult job with seven children ranging in age from one to twelve. Sir Sandford describes in his diaries an amusing account of the Hutchison children eating while dressed only in their underwear in order to keep their good clothes clean.

When she wasn't entertaining, much of Mrs. Hutchison's day was spent in the stone-walled kitchen, where she and staff used the old

## Hutchison House Museum

kitchen tools to prepare goodies baked over the open hearth. This large room was meant for more than just cooking. Here the family ate, worked and washed — themselves and their clothes. On Saturday nights, they would haul a tin tub out of the pantry and set it in front of the fire for the warmest possible bath.

The doctor's life was not an easy one. He covered a large territory — roughly 260 square kilometers (100 square miles) from Rice Lake to Chemong — in a buggy or, when roads were unfit, on horseback. He was called to the scene of many farm accidents and also did a great deal of obstetric work. Today we shiver with horror when we hear of the then acceptable obstetric practices, which included a program of purging, blistering and bleeding for women about to give birth. Among the doctor's patients were the well-known sisters Catharine Parr Traill and Susanna Moodie.

In the study at the front of the house, visitors can see the saddlebag into which he loaded vials of medicine and instruments for his house calls. Other interesting medical paraphernalia includes a field kit supposedly from the Battle of Waterloo, twigs used to make quinine and a glass mortar to grind compounds for medicines.

Though the Hutchison house has a cosy, comfortable feeling, it is clear that the family was not wealthy. The doctor was often paid in barter, accepting a chicken or a pig for his services. The furnishings are simple: thrifty lengths of Kidderminster carpet were sewn together to create the impression of an attractive rug, and stenciled folk motifs covered the economical pine chairs.

Because the house was built as a joint effort by local volunteers, working at night by the light of bonfires, it is filled with little architectural quirks. Ornamental moldings in the parlour are detailed, but all slightly differently. Door frames in the parlour were cut in such a way that an extra piece was needed to make them fit.

During summer months Hutchison House serves delightful Scottish teas on the terrace overlooking the period gardens. The gardens, though modest in size, have particular historic value. An herb garden contains plants that Mrs. Hutchison may well have used both in cooking and in scenting closets. English daisies and trilliums typify the blend of Old and New World plants.

Visitors may want to combine a trip to Hutchison House with a visit to Lang Pioneer Village (page 46) or the Trent Severn Lift Locks (page 117).

*if you go*

DIRECTIONS: Hutchison House is at 270 Brock St. in Peterborough. From Highway 401 drive north on Highway 115, which becomes the Parkway, to Clonsilla St., where you turn east. Continue as it becomes Charlotte St., then turn north on Rubidge St. to Brock, where you turn east.

SCHEDULE: January to March by appointment. April closed. May through October, Tuesday to Sunday 1 to 5 p.m. November and December, Tuesday to Friday 9 a.m. to 5 p.m., weekends 1 to 5 p.m.

ADMISSION: Adults $1.50, students and seniors $1, children 50 cents.

INFORMATION: Call (705) 743-9710

MAP REFERENCE: 4

## *Laura Secord Homestead, Queenston*

High atop his Niagara Escarpment plinth, the statue of Maj. Gen. Sir Isaac Brock, a tribute to the battle-stricken hero, overlooks peaceful vineyards and parklands. Beneath his shadow, a much humbler monument chronicles the arduous life of a heroine who almost slipped into oblivion.

Although Laura Secord's dangerous 30-km (19-mile) trek to warn British soldiers of an impending American attack was not recognized until many years after the War of 1812, the heroine finally received popular recognition when a candy company took up her good name. The company also restored her 1803 Queenston home to its original condition and now operates it as a museum that provides a more interesting insight into the turbulent history of 1812 Niagara than any commemorative statue.

The pretty portrait on the famous chocolate box shows a delicate young girl, but the real Laura Secord was a busy mother of five at the outset of the war (two more children were to follow). Although her husband, James, was a rising merchant, there seems to be no indication that the Secords had any servants, so while soldiers practiced military manoeuvres, Laura likely spent much of her day at work in the kitchen.

Costumed guides take visitors into the sunny kitchen where she would have toiled in front of the hearth. A curious collection of kitchen gadgets has been assembled to show how women of the day cooked everything from toast to tea cakes over an open fire.

Cuttings from Laura Secord's original moss roses now bloom in the gardens surrounding her white clapboard house. Carefully restored, it is rich in period detail, from the rippled, handmade glass windowpanes down to the pine floorboards held in place with square-head nails. Antique buffs will appreciate the fine collection of Upper Canadian furnishings that includes many unusual items, like a flip-top table that turns into a thronelike chair.

Not entirely without niceties, the Secords were probably prosperous enough to own a set of imported bone china and a silver tea service like the one displayed in the parlour. Guides proudly point out such precious pieces as a tiger's-eye maple desk and a cribbage board made from a walrus tusk.

Upstairs, bedrooms offered comfort without luxury: a pine four-poster and a feather tick mattress for the parents and a small double bed for three or four children to huddle in together on winter nights.

The real interest at the homestead, though, is Laura herself. Visitors have been known to get into some heated discussions on the subject of Laura's famous hike. Some people claim that the Canadian heroine was actually a U.S. traitor — after all, she was born in Massachusetts and was the daughter of a U.S. militia officer. Others say it was understandable that Laura would side with the British — after all, her husband was wounded at Queenston Heights, and while she was searching the battlefield for him U.S. soldiers pillaged the family home.

Popular mythology has it that Laura took along a cow to provide an

*if you go*

**LAURA SECORD HOMESTEAD**

DIRECTIONS: The Laura Secord Homestead is on Partition St. in the village of Queenston, just off the Niagara Parkway, halfway between Niagara Falls and Niagara-on-the-Lake.

SCHEDULE: Tours are conducted daily from mid-May to Labour Day, 10 a.m. to 6 p.m.

ADMISSION: $1.

INFORMATION: Call (416) 262-4851. Tours can be booked in advance through the Laura Secord shop in Niagara Falls, telephone (416) 357-4020.

MAP REFERENCE: 13

**NIAGARA HISTORICAL SOCIETY MUSEUM**

DIRECTIONS: The museum is in Niagara-on-the-Lake at 43 Castlereagh St.

SCHEDULE: Open year-round. May to October daily 10 a.m. to 5 p.m. November, December, March and April daily 1 to 5 p.m. January and February, weekends 1 to 5 p.m. or by appointment.

ADMISSION: Adults $2, students $1, children under 12 50 cents.

INFORMATION: Call (416)468-3912.

MAP REFERENCE: 13

## Laura Secord Homestead

excuse to cross enemy lines, since cattle were free to roam. More likely, though, Laura's companion was not a cow but her niece Elizabeth. Elizabeth, however, could not keep up with her strong aunt. After 30 km (19 miles), Laura stumbled into an Indian camp where the chief helped guide her to Lieutenant FitzGibbon of the British forces. With Laura's warning the British and Indian allies were able to intercept the invading Americans.

More of Laura Secord's possessions, including some silver spoons and a patchwork quilt, can be seen at the Niagara Historical Society Museum, one of the country's oldest museums. It is modest but charming red-brick Edwardian building, and it contains close to 20,000 fascinating artifacts, including Maj. Gen. Sir Isaac Brock's cocked hat dating from the War of 1812. Although Brock was killed before the ostrich-plumed hat ever arrived, it was used at two of his four funerals. The general's body was moved on several occasions for new monuments until 1853, when it arrived at its present resting place in the towering Brock Monument.

Anyone interested in the War of 1812 should visit Fort George while in the Niagara region (see page 49).

## Whitehern, Hamilton

All the opulent clutter of a well-to-do Victorian home has been carefully restored in Hamilton's historic Whitehern. The stone mansion at Jackson and MacNab streets was once the property of Dr. Calvin McQuesten, who made a fortune in one of Hamilton's earliest foundries, the first to manufacture a threshing machine. The house and the original furnishings were donated to the city in the late 1950s by McQuesten's descendants.

Built in 1848, Whitehern was home to three generations of the McQuesten family. Unlike Hamilton's other great house, Dundurn Castle (see page 198), built by that colourful and well-connected Tory Sir Allan MacNab, Whitehern shows a certain restraint. Although he was probably as rich as, or even richer than, the powerful MacNab, McQuesten maintained a much more modest lifestyle. His house is an elegant but not lavish stone residence. One look into the drawing room and visitors can see this was not a party home. Although the red velvet and satin curtains with their gold tassels set a rich tone, the room's scale and furnishings are more suited to entertaining the minister and his wife than holding a gala affair.

Across the hall from the drawing room is a library whose shelves hold nearly 2,000 books. The books offer insight into the three generations that collected them: lots of biblical literature, poetry and gardening books. Dr. Calvin McQuesten kept a wonderful garden, sending away for varieties of seed not commonly available in Canada so that he could introduce new fruit trees to his garden.

A guide dressed as the McQuestens' maid leads visitors through the house, talking about items of particular interest. The Victorian love of accumulation is seen in the dining room's numerous collections of silver and porcelain, including the monogrammed McQuesten family china on the linen-draped table. The sheer volume of china is impressive: about seven sets, plus collections of cut glass, pressed glass, etched glass and crackle glassware, along with turn-of-the-century Wedgwood and enough silver to open an antique shop.

## Whitehern

Afternoon tea would have been taken in the morning room, a casual room that became the repository for all the old furniture. These cast-offs include such valuable items as an 1825 mahogany Chippendale secretary from England.

Upstairs, bedrooms look much as they did when used by later generations of McQuestens, complete with perfume bottles and hat pins on the dressers. Back bedrooms contain display cases filled with the family's paraphernalia, including toys found during the restoration and an unusually valuable silver wine cooler the family used as a flower vase.

The best-known member of the family was T. B. McQuesten, who died in 1948. As Ontario's minister of highways in the Mitchell Hepburn government, he was responsible for building the Queen Elizabeth Way and establishing the Royal Botanical Gardens (see page 175). He may also be due recognition for another popularized development, the family rec room: he finished the basement at Whitehern with pine paneling and overstuffed sofas.

It is always fun to compare homes, and Dundurn Castle (see page 198) also welcomes visitors to see the lifestyle of one of the city's most outrageous and influential characters, Sir Allan MacNab.

---

### *if you go*

**DIRECTIONS:** Whitehern is at the corner of Jackson St. W. and MacNab St. S. in downtown Hamilton. From the Queen Elizabeth Way take Highway 403 into Hamilton. Exit at Main St. E., follow Main to MacNab, and drive south 1 block.

**SCHEDULE:** Open daily year-round. Fall, winter and spring 1 to 4 p.m. Summer, 11 a.m. to 4 p.m.

**ADMISSION:** Adults $2, students and seniors $1.50, children under 5 free.

**INFORMATION:** Call (416) 522-5664

**MAP REFERENCE:** 12

## Barnum House Museum, Grafton

Also known as the Heritage Highway, the stretch of Highway 2 that winds through farm country from Cobourg to Brighton is one of the prettiest routes in the province. Although motorists in a hurry often bypass the route in favor of the faster Highway 401, those with time to spare are well rewarded by the slower, more southerly route that meanders past aging apple orchards and historic homes. This is one of the earliest areas of the province to be settled, and many historic buildings still stand.

One of the oldest and most impressive is Barnum House, an elegant neo-Classical home built about 1819 for an enterprising immigrant, Eliakim Barnum. Barnum House shows that early Canadian houses were not always log cabins in the bush. Barnum clearly lived in high style in his fifteen-room mansion complete with ballroom.

He was likely among the U.S. immigrants often referred to as "late Loyalists." Unlike the original Loyalists, who came north during the American Revolution, these late Loyalists arrived a decade or two later, motivated by free or cheap land rather than loyalty to the crown.

Once in his new country, Barnum quickly put his enterprising talents to work, operating a tavern and a small distillery. By 1830 he had accumulated more than 360 hectares (900 acres) of farmland and had opened a milling business. After his rented house burned down in 1814 he set about building the stately new replacement, well suited to his now prosperous status.

Carpenters were brought in from Vermont to construct the home of white pine. Held together with wooden pegs and hand-hewn beams, the house had some uncommon luxuries, including fireplaces both upstairs and down, as well as a high-ceilinged second story, and a spacious attic.

Barnum likely designed the house himself, in which case he was certainly a man ahead of his time. In an era when clothes, dishes and other household goods were stored in wardrobes and buffets, Barnum cleverly installed closets and cupboards. Excavations of the surrounding grounds have revealed exactly what style of dishes was stored in those

## Barnum House Museum

cupboards: a costly Enoch Blue pattern, imported from England.

Such imported luxuries were not out of the ordinary for this enterprising man. Unfortunately, though, Barnum seems to have spent more time on bookkeeping than diary-keeping. Little is known about him other than that he was a loyal Tory who helped found St. George's Anglican Church in Grafton as well as the town's first public school. He served in the militia, eventually becoming lieutenant-colonel of the Third and Durham.

Research and restoration have been going on for several years to return the house to its early grandeur. Visitors are invited to tour rooms furnished with items contributed by generous local donors. The kitchen has now been fully restored and furnished with reproductions. A second-floor nursery has been painted 1835-style in dark salmon hues and contains some antique toys.

The museum has an impressive collection of clothing (200 pieces and accessories) including the 1825 christening gown of Eliakim's daughter Sarah. The collection is displayed in a new gallery, part of a recent addition to the house.

Barnum's elegant house was one of the earliest examples of early nineteenth-century prosperity in the area. To get a sense of the optimism that stirred local folk in those days, a drive to neighbouring Cobourg is in order. Grafton society would have made the 10-km (6-mile) journey to Cobourg to partake of social gatherings. It was a prosperous port town that had potential to become a hub of commerce. So confident of future greatness were Cobourg's residents that they built a grand Palladian-style town hall, known as Victoria Hall. The building has three lavish stories embellished with carved stone lyres, dolphins and Corinthian columns, all crowned with a cupola. Its construction was a megaproject that nearly bankrupted the town. Today Victoria Hall is still the centre of the community, with its cupola visible above the streetscape as you enter town along Highway 2. Once nearly demolished, it has been restored and is now open to visitors.

## if you go

**BARNUM HOUSE MUSEUM**

DIRECTIONS: Barnum House Museum is on the north side of Highway 2, 10 km (6 miles) east of Cobourg. Cobourg is approximately 80 km (50 miles) east of Metro Toronto.

SCHEDULE: Open year-round. Victoria Day to Labour Day, Wednesday to Sunday 10 a.m. to 4 p.m. In the fall, Wednesday to Sunday 1 to 4 p.m. After January 1, weekdays 1 to 4 p.m.

ADMISSION: Adults $1.50, seniors and students $1, children 50 cents, children under 5 free.

INFORMATION: Call (416) 349-2656

MAP REFERENCE: 3

**VICTORIA HALL**

DIRECTIONS: Victoria Hall is at 55 King St. W. in Cobourg.

SCHEDULE: Open daily year-round during office hours. Tours should be arranged in advance.

ADMISSION: Free.

INFORMATION: Call the Cobourg Chamber of Commerce at (416) 372-5831.

MAP REFERENCE: 3

## Stephen Leacock Home, Orillia

Once reviled by the citizens of the town on Lake Couchiching, Stephen Leacock's name is now a source of pride to Orillia. In fact Orillia now calls itself "The Sunshine Town" after the fame it earned as the locale for Leacock's celebrated satire of life in smalltown Canada, *Sunshine Sketches of a Little Town*.

Leacock's lovely summer home was restored in the 1960s and now receives many visitors who come to browse through the lakeside house laden with Leacock's papers and personal effects, the largest archival holding of Leacock's works.

Those who know Leacock primarily for comic *Sunshine Sketches* might be surprised to learn that he was a professor of economics and political science at McGill University in Montreal, and the first of his sixty-one books was a serious tome called *Elements of Political Science*, written in 1905. He was also a master of languages, fluent in French, Latin, Spanish, German, Greek, Italian and Russian — as well as English.

The present house, completed in 1928, four years after his wife's death, was frequently filled with friends and relatives. Although Leacock had only one child, he enjoyed writing and staging plays for youngsters right in his living room, with blankets strung up for backdrops and posters painted to advertise the young troupe known as the Old Brewery Players. The name refers to the body of water, Brewery Bay, on which Leacock's house is built, near the ruins of a brewery. Leacock was said to have liked the name for its ability "to make people feel thirsty by correspondence as far away as Nevada." Leacock liked a drink and campaigned vigorously, and humourously, against prohibition.

From the ample veranda, the lawn slopes down to the bay, past manicured gardens and shady maples. Leacock once farmed the land, keeping detailed accounts of expenditures and productivity, which enabled him to conclude that one Thanksgiving turkey cost him $100.

The home's fir-paneled rooms are filled with books, manuscripts and correspondence that Leacock-philes can easily spend hours poring over. During summer months five guides are on hand to point out the highlights; at other times there is a curator. Among the highlights is a letter from F. Scott Fitzgerald, who wrote in 1917, when he was the editor of a Princeton literary magazine, asking Leacock to look at a copy in the hope "you'll get one smile out of it for every dozen laughs I got from the Snoopopathes." A first edition of Robert Benchley's *Of All Things* is signed with the message, "To Stephen Leacock, who certainly ought to like most of the stuff in this book as he wrote it himself first." Visitors invariably get a laugh out of Leacock's filing system: one folder is bluntly labeled "Letters from damn fools."

Throughout the house are Orillia artifacts that inspired the Leacock wit, among them the bell hanging on the porch, which once rang the call to abandon ship on the *Enterprise*, the pleasure ship that is said to have inspired Leacock's story of the *Mariposa Belle* and her comic sinking.

The pretty stucco house conveys an atmosphere as light and breezy as Leacock's humour. Sunshine pours in through numerous French doors; the sundial on the lawn is inscribed "I count none but sunny hours."

The second-floor Mariposa Room pays tribute to Leacock's most famous creation, Mariposa, a literary caricature of Orillia and its citizenry

---

### if you go

**DIRECTIONS:** The Stephen Leacock Home is in Orillia off Highway 12B. From Highway 11 take the second Orillia interchange, follow 12B east and look for the signs.

**SCHEDULE:** The home is open daily from April 15 to December 15, Monday to Friday, 10 a.m. to 5 p.m. The home begins to open on weekends from May 24 to Thanksgiving but hours vary so call ahead to confirm. December 15 to April 15 open daily Monday to Friday, 10 a.m. to 3 p.m. or by appointment.

**ADMISSION:** Adults $3, seniors $2.50, youths $1, children 50 cents.

**INFORMATION:** Call (705) 326-9357

**CRUISES:** The *Island Princess*'s two-hour cruises depart from the Orillia town dock during the summer. Adults $12, children $6. (705) 325-2628.

**MAP REFERENCE:** 9

## Stephen Leacock Home

in his collection of short stories *Sunshine Sketches of a Little Town*. Quotations and cartoons of some of the more notable and recognizable send-ups on display include Rev. Rupert Drone, "the innocent and ineffectual rector of the Anglican Church," Jeff Thorpe, the barber whose lucky strike in mining stocks was taken as evidence of his great skill and insight, and Judge Pepperleigh, whose beautiful daughter supplied the stories' love interest.

If a visit to the house inspires an interest in light-hearted cruises, a short drive to the Orillia town dock is a must. There the *Island Princess*, a 230-passenger boat, takes two daily cruises through Lake Couchiching waters, past quiet coves, busy resorts and Native burial grounds. Plans are afoot to drop passengers at Leacock's house, possibly as soon as 1992.

# Alexander Graham Bell Homestead, Brantford

Pretty as a storybook creation, the Bell family's homestead looks more like a happy middle-class home than a hotbed of invention. Yet behind the white picket fence and the trees full of birds is the home and workshop where Alexander Graham Bell developed one of the great technological advancements of our time, the telephone.

Visitors to the Bell Homestead soon learn that Alexander could easily have died long before he invented anything. Born in Scotland to a family long interested in speech sciences, Bell lost two of his brothers to tuberculosis. His parents, realizing that young Alexander's health was threatened too, emigrated to Canada, where they settled on the outskirts of Brantford.

Now a National Historic Site, their house is a museum chronicling Bell's many inventions as well as revealing his family's nineteenth-century lifestyle. Built in 1858, the white stucco house was bought by the Bells in 1870. During the eleven eventful years the Bells lived here, Alexander worked on some of the major tests and advancements in the telephone, including the world's first long-distance telephone call in 1876, between Brantford and Paris — Paris, Ontario, that is.

When Bell's father sold the house in 1881, most of the furnishings were auctioned off. It was nearly three decades later that locals realized the historic value of the home and began hunting for the Bell furniture. Luckily, most of the pieces had remained in the area.

Now many of the original furnishings have been returned to the home, including an elegant inlaid table, family portraits and a table unfortunately made from the family piano. In a sunny parlour with lace-draped windows and tasseled draperies, a photo album lies open and a basket of half-finished embroidery looks recently abandoned. The hearing tube resting on a fireside chair once belonged to Alexander's mother and is an important artifact in the story of the telephone's development. His mother's deafness no doubt provided an inspiration for Bell to continue his father's work in speech studies, and it was this work that led Bell both to his bride, Mabel, and to ideas for the telephone.

## *Alexander Graham Bell Homestead*

The inventor's study holds a few pieces of early telephone equipment, including a transmitter, and a storybook Bell wrote as an aid for instructing deaf children. Extra-heavy script was used to show children how to emphasize the words they couldn't hear. More surprising is the stuffed duck-billed platypus sitting on Bell's bookshelf. Apparently a cousin who visited Australia thought it would be a swell gift for Bell. That was not the only stuffed animal Bell received: his wife thought a stuffed owl was an appropriate comment on the inventor's nocturnal hours. Bell apparently enjoyed spending days with his family and consequently worked late into the night.

Visitors are welcome to explore the house at their own pace. Well-placed signs point out items of interest, and a staff member is on hand to answer questions. Visitors are bound to be impressed by the scope of the inventor's interests. Bell worked on an innovative hydrofoil (the fastest boat of its day) and several heavier-than-air flying machines such as the 1909 Silver Dart biplane.

A neighboring clapboard house on the property was Bell's first telephone office. Here Rev. Thomas Henderson gave up God's service to become Bell's agent. The promise was simple and awesome: "The Telephone. For cheap and quick communication, by direct speech. Time and distance overcome." All for $20 a year.

Among the prototype telephones and other gadgetry displayed in this historic first phone office is some of the early gear used by switchboard operators as they tended the lines at

---

### *if you go*

**DIRECTIONS:** The Bell Homestead is at 94 Tutela Heights Rd., south of Brantford. From downtown follow the blue telephone signs to the museum. Brantford is about 30 km (19 miles) west of Hamilton. From the Queen Elizabeth Way, exit at Highway 403 and continue west.

**SCHEDULE:** Open daily mid-June to Labour Day 10 a.m. to 6 p.m. During remainder of the year open Tuesday to Sunday 10 a.m. to 5 p.m.

**ADMISSION:** Free, but donations are appreciated.

**INFORMATION:** Call (519) 756-6220

**MAP REFERENCE:** 15

the rear of the local post office or general store. Early headsets weighed 3 kg (6 1/2 pounds) and had to be strapped over the shoulders like a harness — it's not surprising that they were manufactured at a livery stable.

# Woodside National Historic Site, Kitchener

Although William Lyon Mackenzie King, Canada's longest-serving prime minister, lived in this attractive brick house only briefly during his youth, he remembered his Woodside years as the days "that left the most abiding of all impressions and most in the way of family association."

Today, visitors get a strong sense of what life was like in the King household as they tour the late-Victorian residence restored with period furnishings and many of the family's prized possessions. (The furnishings are all accurate, we know, because King assisted during the planning for the restoration.) The Canadian Parks Service, which administers Woodside, does an admirable job of communicating the spirit of the day through costumed guides who are well informed about the family and the customs and furnishings of the period.

Looking much as it probably did in 1891, when Mackenzie King was sixteen, the house is fairly typical for an aspiring middle-class family of that time. King's father, John, was a lawyer just starting out in Kitchener with a wife who epitomized the Victorian lady. Isabel King was a renowned hostess and local socialite who overspent her husband's budget, thanks to her love of clothes.

Although this comfortable ten-room residence, rented by the Kings for seven years, is not lavish, its furnishings illustrate Victorian love of opulence.

The dining room afforded ample opportunity to show off elaborate manners and fine possessions to a guest given the choice seat at the table, close to the warmth of the wood stove, facing the shelves where a silver coffee urn, cruets and cake plates were all proudly displayed.

The parlour was the place where Victorians showed their prosperity, and it usually remained closed except for special occasions or the arrival of guests. Oriental vases, floral wallpaper borders and lace curtains set the stage for entertaining. Sofas are draped with antimacassars and lamps are shaded with puffs of pink fabric and delicate lace. This stuff wasn't just decorative: the antimacassars protected the furniture from hair slicked with bear grease, as was the fashion of the day, and the lace-covered shades hid sooty buildup in kerosene lamps. On the walls are photos of the King family. A large rectangular piano is strategically placed within view of the kitchen so Mrs. King could keep an eye on daughters practicing at the keyboard.

The library is the most comfortable room of the house and the equivalent of the modern-day family room, where the family played cards, read, sewed and enjoyed games of checkers and chess. However, the King children did not have a great deal of spare time. William and his brother Max had plenty of chores, including chopping the wood that fueled the five wood stoves in the house. The Kings seemed to have a chronic problem keeping hired help, and the girls were often called upon to help with the housework and cooking.

The kitchen's cast-iron cook stove, elaborately decorated in full rococo glory, was an all-purpose appliance that included a reservoir for heating water. Here guides often bake from period receipes, making seasonal goodies like a white Christmas fruitcake from one of Mrs. King's own recipes. They'll often hand out copies of the recipe to visitors.

Visitors who are familiar with Mackenzie King's diaries invariably look for boyhood evidence of his fascination with the occult. But for a man who enjoyed communing with other worlds, there are no signs of any unusual obsession here. Instead, guides talk about a typical teenage boy who stole plums from a teacher's tree and knocked over an outhouse. His bedroom upstairs looks entirely ordinary. His original bed has been restored. Hanging on the wall are drawings of dogs sketched by his mother, an accomplished artist.

The Kings wrote reams of letters

---

*if you go*

DIRECTIONS: Woodside National Historic Site is at 528 Wellington St. N. in Kitchener. From Highway 401 take Highway 8 west. Follow the beaver signs on King St. when Highway 8 becomes King St.

SCHEDULE: Open daily year-round 10 a.m. to 5 p.m.

ADMISSION: Free.

INFORMATION: Call (519) 742-5273

MAP REFERENCE: 16

## Woodside National Historic Site

to each other and their penchant for saving every little thing has left historians with a rich legacy of anecdotes to cull from, enabling guides to talk with such familiarity about the King family that it soon seems to visitors as if they are old friends.

The Canadian Parks Service stages many special events throughout the year, each time decorating the house appropriately. These events include a July 1 Garden Party. During the Christmas season the house is at its loveliest, festooned with greenery and with the dining table set for a grand feast.

# Parkwood, Oshawa

Oshawa's oasis of opulence is a magnificent mansion set in 5 hectares (12 acres) of manicured grounds. Parkwood was formerly the home of industrialist Colonel R. S. McLaughlin and his wife, Adelaide. McLaughlin pioneered the automotive industry in Canada and eventually merged his successful and innovative McLaughlin Carriage Works with General Motors. Through his inventiveness and business acumen he amassed a fortune and not only built this lavish estate but also funded many charities and community projects.

After McLaughlin's death in 1972 at the age of 101, Parkwood was left to the local hospital and run by a foundation to earn money through its tours. McLaughlin's daughters, who had inherited the furnishings, kindly left them in place so that visitors see the house much as it was when the automotive magnate resided there. In fact it is the furnishings that make the place so interesting, since they suggest much about the man who built the place. Now volunteer guides lead visitors through about thirty of the fifty-five rooms.

Although the main house was constructed between 1915 and 1917, there were many later changes and additions. In the 1920s the main hall was painted with murals depicting woodlands, and during the Great Depression an open porch was enclosed to create a sunroom — as well as jobs.

Amid the splendor of the sunroom is a well-worn armchair, the most modest piece of furniture in the house: it is said to have been McLaughlin's favourite spot for lounging. Guides sometimes tell the story of how in the lonely days after his wife died he would sit near the window for its view of the huge fir tree that was lavishly decorated at Christmas. When people stopped to look at the tree, he ran out to talk to them.

Walking into the drawing room, full of French baroque flourishes, is a glorious experience. A sylvan scene is painted inside the lid of a gilded Steinway grand piano, and a centuries-old tapestry of Greek goddesses hangs on one wall. Priceless antiques are everywhere. Despite the grandeur, though, this still feels like someone's home. The ornamental top of the McLaughlins' 1878 wedding cake still sits in the drawing

## Parkwood

room's china cabinet.

Portraits of the family hang on the silk-damask-covered dining-room walls, surrounding a table that could be expanded to seat twenty-two. Guests who stayed for a week might never dine from the same dishes twice, since the family owned seven complete sets of china.

As guides go through the rooms they rattle off by rote lists of Chippendale tables, Louis XV chairs, exotic eighteenth-century Chinese goldfish tanks, and rare what-nots. But there is so much to mention that it all begins to sound like an inventory list after a while. The things that really interest are the personal items. On the second floor visitors enter the private realm of the family. The McLaughlin daughters might have lived in a world of dinner parties and servants, but their mother still wanted them to learn how to cook. She had a small second-floor kitchen installed. The adjoining playroom is now a little gallery filled with changing art exhibits.

Even the bedrooms are seen on the guided tour. Visitors get to look into the colonel's shoe cupboard. An Art Deco bedroom looks frozen in time. At the bedside is a copy of *The Last Spike*, which McLaughlin was reading when he died, as well as an oversize cup and saucer to hold the teakettle broth he drank every night — a mixture of hot buttered squares of toast with warm milk, onions and garlic.

A sense of play permeates the great house. From the sunroom McLauglin could use control panels to illuminate the gardens and turn on the powerful player organ that had 100 rolls of music. Just off the main hallway is a full-size bowling alley complete with automated pin setter, as well as a typically masculine billiard room complete with a 1,125-kg (2,500-pound) English billiard table and wall murals of McLaughlin's sporting life: fishing, hunting and sailing. The McLaughlins and their guests could also enjoy the indoor pool and squash court.

If the tour fuels fantasies of a luxurious lifestyle, visitors can indulge themselves, during the summer season, with lunch or afternoon tea in the magnificent gardens. In the grounds visitors stroll past massive spruce, chestnut and maple trees, through glens dotted with statuary and through formal gardens with a 75-m (83-foot) reflecting pool beside which the tea house serves refreshments. It is a rare opportunity to sit back in the calm of a lovely mansion and drift momentarily into that lifestyle most of us can only ever dream about.

To further explore Oshawa's automotive history, a visit to the Canadian Automotive Museum is recommended (see page 148).

*if you go*

DIRECTIONS: Parkwood is at 270 Simcoe St. N. in Oshawa. From Highway 401 take Exit 417 north onto Simcoe St.

SCHEDULE: Open Tuesday to Sunday and holiday Mondays June through September 10:30 a.m. to 4 p.m. The rest of the year Tuesday to Friday and Sunday 1:30 to 4 p.m.

ADMISSION: Adults $6, seniors and students $4, family $15, children under 5 free.

INFORMATION: Call (416) 579-1311

TEA HOUSE: Open June through Labour Day.

MAP REFERENCE: 6

## *Macaulay Heritage Park, Picton*

Picton's Macaulay Heritage Park is not a grand affair — just a lovely Georgian house and church — but it speaks eloquently of the early days of a Loyalist town and the sensibilities of those who influenced it, a sort of museum equivalent of a Jane Austen novel.

Visitors walking into the house are often greeted with the warm, yeasty smell of bread baking in the brick ovens. (Local people in the know pop in to buy the still-warm loaves of whole-wheat bread, often baked on Sunday afternoons.) A guide, dressed suitably for the part of the Macaulays' nineteenth-century cook, might be rolling out Welsh cakes to bake on the griddle over an open fire, but she'll take time out from her baking to talk about the Macaulay family and show visitors around the house.

The son of a Kingston merchant and Loyalist, William Macaulay inherited 200 hectares (500 acres) in the Picton area (then known as Hallowell Bay) on his father's death in 1800. The young Macaulay was only six at the time, but several years later, after studying in Oxford, he came back to the area to offer his services as a newly ordained Anglican minister and missionary. Not many missionaries would have had Macaulay's financial resources — he was able to build an attractive stone church and the rather lovely two-story house next door.

Macaulay might have been educated in the way of the Lord, but he also showed a great deal of natural ability in more earthly matters. He donated land for the courthouse and jail in the hope of making Picton the county seat — and he succeeded. He sold land for a token $1 to the nearby Roman Catholic church to advance development in the area where he owned land. When others wanted to name the area Port William after the king, Macaulay was intent on naming it Picton after General Sir Thomas Picton, second in command in the Battle of Waterloo, where he was killed in action. With a brother on the executive council of the Legislative Assembly, Macaulay prevailed.

He was certainly an important man in the community, and this gracious brick house reflects his social standing. A look into the front parlour reveals an early upright piano imported from England. The Macaulays had the first such instrument in the county, a wedding present received at the time of William's first marriage. After his wife's death he remarried in 1853 and had some remodeling done on the house; marble fireplaces, for instance, replaced the old wood-burning hearths in the parlour and the dining room. This is the period to which the house has been restored.

A grand dining room reflects the family's grand entertaining. They loved cards and had a wine cellar under the front door. Though this way of life was not typical of most missionaries, the Macaulays certainly were well positioned to enjoy some of life's luxuries, and the Anglican Church did not frown upon them. Macaulay was even known to write to his mother requesting "several bottles of good Madeira for a clerical meeting."

In his study is a marble bust of his beloved General Picton, along with an engraving of the explorer Sir John Franklin. The second Mrs. Macaulay's brother was an ensign on the fatal Franklin expedition in search of a northwest passage.

The neighboring church that Macaulay built is also part of the park and was converted to a museum in 1973 to tell the history of Prince Edward County. The chancel has been lovingly restored, complete with original decorative wall stencils, and the 1854 tracker organ is still heard in the occasional concert.

Old photos and artifacts make a fascinating chronicle of local development: photos depict a bustling Picton harbour that was a busy fishing and shipping port. From the 1860s to the 1890s the barley boom saw tons of

> **if you go**
>
> DIRECTIONS: The Macaulay Heritage Park is at Church and Union streets in Picton. From Belleville drive south on Highway 62, then east on Highway 33 (Main St.). Turn south at Union Street.
>
> SCHEDULE: From May 1 to Labour Day, weekdays 10 a.m. to 4:30 p.m., weekends 1 to 4:30 p.m. Closed Tuesdays. Fall and winter, call first.
>
> ADMISSION: Free, but donations are appreciated.
>
> INFORMATION: Call (613) 476-3833
>
> MAP REFERENCE: 2

## Macaulay Heritage Park

grain shipped south to U.S. breweries. But when U.S. tariffs squelched the trade in 1894, the issue of free trade was hotly debated — a debate as old as the country itself. Around the turn of the century the county made the transition to other types of agriculture, namely fruits and vegetables.

With its bountiful farms, the county saw some prosperity in the form of canning factories, two of which remain in business today. The display of old can labels is made particularly interesting by the knowledge that early Group of Seven artists got their start in design work, painting pears and green beans for these colourful cans.

While Macaulay might have been the most influential of Picton's early residents, he was not the most famous. Sir John A. Macdonald practiced law here from 1833 to 1835, substituting for his ailing cousin. The young John A. got his political start here too, being elected secretary to the school board. This was also where he earned his first fee and made his first speech to a jury, defending himself on charges of mischief.

The Macdonald family managed a stone mill in nearby Glenora, and it still stands today, just a ten-minute drive east of Picton. It is one of the loveliest spots in Ontario, situated on a particularly scenic stretch of the Bay of Quinte. Here a ferry takes cars and foot passengers back and forth across the bay, linking both ends of Highway 33, also known as the Loyalist Parkway. A busy little restaurant, The Wheelhouse, has an outdoor patio overlooking the water and the ferry, and it's a great place for lunch. For a spectacular view, head up the hill to Lake on the Mountain Conservation Area, where an unusual mountaintop lake has become a font for all sorts of curious myths — including one that has it connected underground to Niagara Falls.

## Joseph Brant Museum, Burlington

Now in the shadow of apartment towers, highways and a large hospital, Joseph Brant's 1800 home is one of the earliest pioneer settlements in Burlington. The clapboard home is a modest monument to a remarkable man whose success transcended traditional cultural boundaries.

Joseph Brant was born in the Thirteen Colonies in 1742 and spent his childhood in the Mohawk River Valley in New York State. There he met William Johnson, the King of England's representative for Indian Affairs who married his older sister, Molly. Brant was no more than thirteen when he joined Mohawk warriors fighting the French at Fort George. When Brant was nineteen, Johnson, by then knighted for his military successes, enrolled him in a Connecticut school where Natives were encouraged to learn English and act as missionaries.

After his schooling Brant appears to have led a prosperous life as a farmer until the first rumblings of the American Revolution. Brant, by this time a Native leader, resolved to negotiate an alliance with the British and to formalize Native land rights by visiting Britain with the representative of the Department of Indian Affairs in 1775.

Appearing at balls attired in his Native costume, Brant cut a dashing figure that attracted attention throughout London. Boswell wrote about him in the London *Times*, Romney painted his portrait at the request of the Earl of Warwick, and he was invited to become a Mason. At the end of the Revolution, Brant was eventually able to negotiate lands on the Bay of Quinte and along the Grand River for the Six Nations Iroquois, who were made homeless after the American victory. These reserve lands presented problems that kept Brant in negotiations for years. The lands were not large enough to support hunting but were too large to farm, and Brant wanted to sell and lease lots to white settlers. The British argued that the land was given to the Indians in trust, not to be disposed of without official British authorization.

In the last years of his life Brant was granted 1,380 hectares (3,450 acres) of land at the head of the lake, on what today is the Burlington

## Joseph Brant Museum

waterfront. In 1800 he built a gracious two-story home here and spent the rest of his life in relative comfort.

Although the original house eventually fell into ruin, its copy was built on the lakefront site in 1937 and today it houses a museum dedicated to Burlington's heritage. Since Brant is usually acknowledged as Burlington's first citizen, a large part of the museum is devoted to telling his story.

Recent renovations have been made on the ground floor to create two period rooms. One portrays the life of the Six Nations Iroquois with artifacts such as Native tools and ceremonial items like the reproductions of false face masks and the Cayuga condolence cane, carved with pictographs that serve as a memory aid in recounting the hereditary chiefs of the Five Nations during the ceremony at which a new chief was installed.

Joseph Brant's accomplishments are remembered through such precious artifacts as a gilt gorget (a piece of throat-protecting armor) and a red silk banner painted with the coat of arms and presented to him by George III. Other artifacts of his include the ring he bought on his first trip to England and a dress sword.

Brant's library has been reconstructed to show how it might have looked in 1800, with books reflecting tastes encompassing both Georgian and American Federal periods. Furnishings such as the grandfather clock and candlestick table and the glassware would have been imported from England. In its day this two-story home with its clapboard cladding was probably the most impressive structure for miles around, and the museum displays make it clear that Brant enjoyed a genteel life, often with lavish entertaining. One event at the Brant estate was said to have been attended by a 1,000 people.

In comparison to Brant's exciting life, the later stages of Burlington's heritage seem somewhat less spectacular, but the adjoining Burlington History Gallery illustrates the development of Burlington with a few choice artifacts. The second-floor gallery usually displays a few tantalizing pieces, on a rotating basis, from its outstanding costume collection, which at 7,000 articles is said to be second only to the Royal Ontario Museum's collection.

> ### if you go
>
> DIRECTIONS: The Joseph Brant Museum is at 1240 North Shore Blvd. E., in Burlington. From the Queen Elizabeth Way exit at North Shore Blvd. E. Continue east and follow the signs to the hospital. Park in the hospital lot. Take your ticket into the museum to be validated.
>
> SCHEDULE: Open daily year-round, Monday to Saturday 10 a.m. to 5 p.m., Sunday 1 to 5 p.m.
>
> ADMISSION: Adults $2, seniors and students $1.50, children $1.
>
> INFORMATION: Call (416) 634-3556
>
> MAP REFERENCE: 11

*tasty trips*

## *Pick Your Own Fun at Two Ontario Apple Orchards*

In a high-tech, fast-paced world, one family activity really satisfies the urge to get in touch with nature. Pick-your-own farms are becoming increasingly popular as farmers turn their fields and orchards into tourist attractions for people who enjoy a sensuous morning outdoors and getting back to nature gathering their own vine-fresh, sun-ripened fruit — as much as the chance to save a few dollars on the grocery bill. The range of what you can pick is remarkable — everything from apples to zucchini.

Picking your own can be a money-saving venture, but it does take some extra planning if you have young children in tow. Kids love picking all sorts of fruits and vegetables for the same reasons they like visiting farm animals — it lets them feel connected to the living world. But fruit-picking can be tiring and monotonous for some youngsters, so it helps to find a farm that caters to families by providing a little extra entertainment.

During hot summer months, picking experts know that the fruit is best and the work is easiest in the cool morning air. Come prepared with sunscreen, insect repellant, hats, long sleeves or trousers for anything prickly (like raspberries) and a water bottle. Perhaps the most pleasant picking is done in the autumn, when apples are at their peak. The air is crisp and comfortable, and apples are an easy fruit to pick: you can fill up a basket in next to no time and you don't get sticky, stung or pricked in the process. The picking becomes a party at many Ontario orchards that offer wagon rides, cider celebrations and home cooking. One such place is Chudleigh's Apple Farm north of Milton, where families can pick their own fruit in a 29-hectare (72-acre) orchard containing 24,000 apple trees.

Chudleigh's is one of the first farms to take the plunge into agri-tourism, offering entertainment along with the apples. It begins with a wagon ride into the orchards where the fruit grows on dwarf trees — low to the ground for easy picking. Entertainment is well suited to families with young children. There are a few farm animals in the yard — usually puppies, chickens, a duck and a goat — as well as a wonderful haymow where kids who get bored with picking can swing from ropes and tires tied to the rafters and take a tumble in soft mountains of hay.

During summer this is a great place to arrive hungry. Two tents are set up for food service, offering, among other fare, barbecued corn painted with butter. A fire destroyed the bakery that produced Chudleigh's famous apple pies, but the splendid pies are now being made by a local bakery (with Chudleigh's fruit and recipes) and are every bit as good. So good, in fact, that more than 1,000 are made daily, and they are often sold out on busy weekends. It's wise to reserve a pie in advance by telephone. (I recommend the apple pie with crumb topping.)

Children can get their first farm job by helping to gather windfall apples for cider-making. Every child who fills a case gets paid a silver dollar. There's no shortage of eager young helpers on the weekends.

Picking usually begins in mid-September with the McIntosh apples, followed by Spartans and Cortlands. By early October the Red Delicious are ready, followed by Northern Spy, Golden

## *if you go*

**CHUDLEIGH'S APPLE FARM**

**DIRECTIONS:** Chudleigh's Apple Farm is north of Milton, 3 km (2 miles) north of Highway 401 on Highway 25.

**SCHEDULE:** Open daily year-round from 9 a.m. to dark.

**ADMISSION:** Free.

**INFORMATION:** Call (416) 878-2725

**MAP REFERENCE:** 11

**DEVINS ORCHARDS**

**DIRECTIONS:** Devins Orchards is northeast of Toronto on Warden Ave. From Highway 404, drive east on the Aurora Side Rd. to Warden Ave., then south about 1 km (1/2 mile) on Warden.

**SCHEDULE:** Open daily during apple season.

**ADMISSION:** Free.

**INFORMATION:** Call (416) 888-1637

**MAP REFERENCE:** 8

## Pick Your Own Fun at Two Ontario Apple Orchards

Delicious and Russets. Chudleigh's also has a fresh produce stall that sells other fruits and vegetables from local farms.

Although the pick-your-own fun seems to peak during five frantic weekends in late September and early October, Chudleigh's has expanded its orchard events to last from September 1 to June 30. During the winter cross-country skiers shuffle through the orchards, and in spring there are the blossom tours, and planting materials are on sale for gardeners.

To the east of Metro, Devins Orchards is a delightful farm that looks at least as old as the towering pines that shade its long driveway. This is a folksy place where youngsters can watch the miniature horses, deer and rabbits while they wait for the wagon that takes them on a ten-minute hayride to the orchard. Visitors are given plastic bags that hold approximately 9 kg (20 pounds) of apples, which they can fill for about $10. Ladders are already in the orchard for the the serious pickers who like to reach the top boughs of the McIntosh, Greening and Delicious trees. After picking, visitors can buy a snack of homebaked pie, cider or candy apples at the shop.

### THE PICK OF THE PICK-YOUR-OWN

The Ontario Ministry of Agriculture offers a comprehensive listing of more than 300 pick-your-own farms across the province producing everything from peas to pumpkins. Call the Ministry of Tourism and Recreation at 1-800-ONT-ARIO (965-4008 from Toronto) for a free copy of this excellent publication. Before visiting any orchard or farm, be sure to phone ahead; the availability of produce is dependent upon weather and many other variables. These factors can also affect the price.

Several telephone lines provide updates on picking. A weekly Pick-Your-Own report begins in early June and runs through the growing season. It describes the availability of produce in the area from London to Oshawa and is updated weekly. Call (416) 924-6254. Ontario berry growers provide a hotline with the latest crop information from early June to the end of July; call 1-800-263-3262.

## Tyrone Mill, Bowmanville

In many ways, time seems to have stood still in Tyrone, a pretty hamlet north of Bowmanville where water power still operates the mill, as it has since 1846. Here you can sip some freshly squeezed cider while watching another batch of apples being pressed on old-fashioned wooden equipment.

The 1846 mill is the oldest in Durham Region, and although custom-cut lumber has replaced flour as the mill's main business, much of the original equipment is still in place. Cider-pressing, which begins late each September, is done much the same way it was a hundred years ago, according to mill owner Robert Shafer.

In the press room apples are washed before being jiggled up the conveyor to be ground into a pulp called pomace. This applesaucelike mash containing seeds and peels is spread on nylon cloth, in layers separated by oak racks, then squeezed under 15 tonnes of pressure. The resulting juice is filtered, then stored in a refrigerated vat.

Unlike store-bought cider, which is usually clarified and pasteurized, Robert Shafer's variety remains cloudy. Free of preservatives, it will last for a week in the refrigerator before it either ferments into hard (alcoholic) cider or turns to vinegar. It can be frozen for up to a year.

Custom pressing is offered to people who bring their own apples, providing they are of good quality. Rotten and wormy apples can contaminate the equipment.

Apples ripen at different times, so the flavour of cider varies as each new variety arrives. A blend of sweet and tart works best, and one of the best ciders comes at the end of October when McIntoshes are blended with Spys and Russets.

Saturdays and Sunday afternoons till Christmas are the times to see the pressing (which usually begins in mid-September and continues to May) because the staff usually cook cider doughnuts, which they sell with the freshly squeezed cider. On busy autumn weekends a wood-fueled apple drier is outside the front of the mill is used to dehydrate apple slices for winter storage. Homemade pies, tarts, apple dumplings

# Tyrone Mill

and apple butter are all sold in the store, along with Empire cheese from the Campbellford cheese factory. In the fall an unusual cider, half apple and half pear, is sold on weekends.

Shafer scours local farms to find some seldom-seen varieties of apples: Northwest Greens, La Salles, Tolman Sweets, Golden Russets, Cortlands, Baxters, Macouns and Snows — all of which visitors can buy in their uncrushed form.

In recent years Shafer has worked to restore the original grist mill, but the mill stones that once ground the flour now lie in pieces out front. Finding replacements for these behemoth rocks was no easy job, but after years of searching he found stones in old mills in Pennsylvania and New York. Quarried in France many years ago from a dense quartzite called buhrstone, the stones are immense. A runner, or top stone, weighs a little over 2 tonnes and is nearly 1.5 m (5 feet) across. When the stones are ready, Shafer will use water power to grind wheat into whole-wheat flour.

### if you go

**DIRECTIONS:** The Tyrone Mill is at the junction of Concession 7 and Regional Road 14 (Liberty St.), north of Bowmanville. From Highway 401 take the Liberty St. exit and drive north 13 km (8 miles).

**SCHEDULE:** Open year-round, Monday to Saturday 9 a.m. to 6 p.m., Sundays from September through June 1 to 5 p.m. No apple cider during the summer.

**ADMISSION:** Free.

**INFORMATION:** Call (416) 263-8871 to confirm times if you want to see apple-pressing.

**MAP REFERENCE:** 6

## Richters Herbs, Stouffville

Winter winds may be whipping snow across the highway, but inside Richters greenhouse, east of Stouffville, the atmosphere is decidedly springlike. Primrose and mint scent the air and the coltsfoot are already sporting little yellow tufts of bloom. This preview of May is a gardener's delight, but you don't have to be a gardener to appreciate the astounding variety of herbs available here.

Richters is a commercial venture, but with an estimated 500 herbs, this greenhouse seems more like a comprehensive botanical garden. Arranged in alphabetical order, each variety is accompanied by an informative sign so that visitors perusing these pots of greenery get a mini course in botany.

What fascinates visitors at this greenhouse are not the lavish blooms and tropical exotics but the humble herbs put to a myriad of uses. Where else can you shop for herbal remedies for coughs, stomach inflammations and bubonic plague? Those remedies are all said to be found in one plant, saxifrage burnet.

Most visitors are looking not for cures but culinary aids. Richters supplies fresh herbs to several well-known Toronto restaurants, and visitors can supply their own kitchens with both familiar and unusual herbs, either as seeds or as potted plants ready for a sunny window or the garden. Most herbs turn out to have other applications beyond the kitchen.

Sage, known to most cooks as the favourite flavour for a turkey stuffing, comes in some surprising variations. Fruit sage has showy purple blooms that would make it worthwhile as a decorative plant, but its fruit-scented leaves can also be used in potpourris. Painted sage, adorned with delicate red flowers, is said to increase the inebriating effect of alcohol when added during fermentation. But make a tea from it and you can use it as a mouthwash.

Culinary substitutions abound here. Run out of lemon and you can always use some lemon verbena leaves to flavour the sauce instead. People who like the taste of garlic but can't stand what it does to their breath may want to try the garlic chives for a milder after-smell. Anyone

*tasty trips* 103

## Richters Herbs

wanting to cut down sugar intake will be interested in the claims made for sweet cicely, whose leaves and stalks are said to be so sweet that only half the usual amount of sugar is needed in recipes that use it.

Even if they were utterly useless, many of these herbs would be worth growing just for their ornamental value. Particularly pretty are the woody little bushes of Majorca rosemary, whose twisted stems look like bonsai trees. Ditany of Crete is an oregano that could be used in a tomato sauce, except that with its sprays of pink flowers it looks too lovely to disturb.

One doesn't expect to find geraniums in an herb collection, but roughly five dozen varieties are cultivated at Richters, not for their ornamental blooms but for their scented leaves. Brushing the Frensham geranium with fingertips releases a powerful lemon fragrance. Scents of mint, rose, spice, almond and even coconut can be found in fuzzy geranium leaves. As well as simply scenting the air, geranium leaves can be used in cooking, to line a pan filled with cake batter or to flavour a jelly. The citrus-scented varieties were particularly popular during the nineteenth century, when lemons and oranges were too expensive for daily use.

Mrs. Richter and her staff welcome questions from curious visitors and happily share a host of tips on cultivation and cooking. A small gift shop sells lots of herb-related goodies. Highly recommended are the honey scented with lemon verbena, and Mrs. Richter's own blend of herbal tea. A selection of herbal cookbooks is available, but for a really good read try Mrs. Richter's catalogue — it's a compendium of fascinating facts.

### if you go

**DIRECTIONS:** Richters is 1 km (1/2 mile) east of the village of Goodwood on the south side of Highway 47. Goodwood is located roughly 10 km (6 miles) northeast of Stouffville.
**SCHEDULE:** Open daily 8:30 a.m. to 5 p.m. Reduced hours during fall and winter.
**ADMISSION:** Free.
**INFORMATION:** Call (416) 640-6677
**MAP REFERENCE:** 6

## Tasting the Grape on Niagara's Winery Trail

Wine has been made in the Niagara Peninsula for centuries, but only in recent years has it begun to be a source of pride for Canadians. No longer the brunt of jokes for their soda-pop-sweet flavour, Canadian wines have undergone a transformation as growers have learned how to cultivate delicate European vinifera vines in Canada and winemakers have developed techniques to produce wines that hold their own in world tasting competitions.

The region is one of the most scenic in the province, with thousands of hectares of vineyards and orchards. The Niagara Escarpment shelters the area and keeps the moderating influence of Lake Ontario winds circulating between the escarpment and the lake, crating a microclimate that benefits the cultivation of grapes.

Many wineries now welcome visitors to taste their wares. The Niagara Wine Route guides motorists to fourteen wineries and one grape juice processor, with the aid of an illustrated brochure and blue road signs emblazoned with white grapes.

Many of the larger wineries are already well known, for example Bright's, which offers slick tours and tastings at its massive facility in Niagara Falls. But especially interesting are some of the small wineries and grape growers. Stoney Ridge Cellars, near Stoney Ridge, is one such facility, a small winery perched on the Niagara Escarpment. The winery itself is a modest building that accommodates the towering stainless-steel fermentation tanks, though its modest appearance belies the fact that this winery enjoys a very good reputation with oenophiles.

Winemaker Jim Warren is a high-school teacher whose homemade wine has earned him several Canadian amateur championship titles. He went "pro" with a temporary licence in 1985 and produced only 3,785 L (1,000 gallons). In 1986 the winery received its official licence and has grown ever since, now producing 94,635 L (25,000 gallons) a year.

The tour through the facility is short, but visitors will also find it highly personal, particularly on weekends when they may well have a chance to chat with one of the owners. Free tastings include samples of

# Tasting the Grape on Niagara's Winery Trail

roughly half a dozen of the winery's thirty wines, many of which have won international awards, including a silver medal at the International Wine Challenge in London, England, for the Eastman Vineyard Chardonnay.

The oak-paneled tasting room is informal, with local folk frequently popping in to buy grape juice for home winemaking. Visitors will certainly be rewarded with some discoveries, including such wines as Colombard and Mario Muscat that are seldom seen in liquor stores.

Another pleasant surprise along the Wine Route is Wiley Bros. Ltd., grape juice processors, who have run a family farm near St. Catharines for six generations. Clair Wiley estimates that the family business is one of the top five growers in Ontario, with 140 hectares (350 acres) of grapes producing twenty-three varieties.

The juice plant was built in the 1970s, when surpluses led to the loss of vast quantities of grapes, and it has continued to expand since. The machinery bears a remarkable resemblance to a winery's. After all, the process of crushing and destemming is identical. But once the fruit has been processed, the difference begins. The crushed (but not yet pressed) fruit is heated to produce juice, which is then pasteurized and cooled. In a refrigerated room towering stainless-steel tanks hold juice at temperatures below the freezing point of water. The high sugar content prevents freezing.

After touring the juice plant, visitors will likely take a new interest in Ontario grapes and juice. This is grape juice for the connoisseur, and Wiley's shop sells some varieties that are seldom seen on supermarket shelves. Visitors might try a blend of Muscat and Elvira grapes that looks murky brown but tastes sweet and rich. Also available for home winemakers is a wide selection of juice and grapes in season (including the seldom-seen seedless Himrod).

It is impossible to explore even half the wineries on the route in one day; two or three is about the limit. During autumn the stretch of the Niagara Escarpment between Stoney Creek and St. Catharines is recommended for its scenic vistas and abundant fruit stands. During summer months, drive the Niagara Parkway from Niagara-on-the-Lake to Niagara Falls for its pretty parkland and great picnic spots. Wineries along this section include the well-known Inniskillin (famous for its icewines) and Reif (which boasts a wonderful tasting room where visitors can sample a wide selection of the winery's best. Be sure to try the fruity and exotic Siegfried Ribe).

Not to be missed is Château des Charmes, near St. Davids. Although the concrete-block building looks most mundane (nothing like the grand château depicted on the wine label), it offers one of the best wine tours and tastings an oenophile will ever experience. Proprietor Paul Bosc is an innovator who has discovered new methods to cultivate the best of the French viniferas. His taste is impeccable and his wife makes a gracious and knowledgeable hostess in the tasting room.

*if you go*

Before setting out, obtain a copy of the *Niagara Wine Region* brochure outlining the winery route. It is available from the Ministry of Tourism and Recreation and most LCBO outlets.

MAP REFERENCE: 13

# Bruce's Mill Conservation Area Sugar Bush, Stouffville

When the spring sunshine turns March snow to meltwater, the sweetest season of all begins in Southern Ontario. By mid-March most sugar bushes are in operation, many with demonstrations of old-fashioned techniques of making maple syrup: boiling sap in Native log troughs or collecting it in tin pails to boil in an outdoor cauldron.

The annual maple syrup fest is always the highlight of the year at Bruce's Mill, a conservation area northeast of Metro Toronto that is also popular with cross-country skiers, who can glide through the bush to see how trees are tapped using modern-day methods. Plastic tubing, which looks an awful lot like intravenous lines, connects roughly 1,200 trees in the sugar bush. As warm days coax trees into sap production, the lines siphon off the precious fluid, drawing it down to the sugar shack where it is boiled down in the wood-fueled evaporator.

Signs along the sugar bush trail explain the process, and staff are on hand to answer questions about the large-scale operation, explaining how the cryptic markings on trees provide a guide for stringing up the lines of plastic tubing. Armed with free brochures, and with plenty of illustrated signs around, visitors get a mini lesson in the fine art of syrup-making as well as the process of managing a sugar bush.

Long before plastic tubing, evaporators and metal pails, Woodland Indians were making maple syrup by collecting the sap in birchbark containers, then boiling it down in troughs made of hollow logs. Tools used in this process are displayed along the trail, along with a description of the boiling: hot rocks were thrown again and again into the trough of sap until it boiled.

Children are always fascinated by the old-fashioned methods, like the pioneer technique of boiling down sap in a massive cauldron bubbling over an open fire like a witches' brew. To see how early settlers collected the watery sap, visitors can peep into buckets hanging on spiles to see sap dripping from the trees — providing the temperature rises above freezing — and taste the clear fluid, which has only the vaguest hint of sweetness. As much as 152 L (40 gallons) of sap have to be boiled down to make 1 L (1/4 gallon) of syrup.

By comparison modern evaporators seem a breeze to operate. You can walk into the steamy shack, where even the air seems sticky with syrup, to watch staff at work, boiling down the sap in a large, open pan over a wood fire, then finishing it over a more easily controlled propane flame. For a really sweet treat, the staff take warm syrup outside and drizzle it onto the snow, where it soon congeals into a sticky maple taffy, a confection that is almost guaranteed to undo any dental work.

Visitors can gorge on pancakes, sausages and syrup at the chalet, then take a horsedrawn wagon ride around the parking lot (on weekends and March break). Be warned: on a pleasant day this place gets really busy, so be prepared to wait for both the pancakes and the ride.

The 1858 mill after which the park was named has been restored, and you can take a walking tour through it. During winter you can sometimes skate on the millpond.

The maple syrup activities usually continue to the first weekend in April. Even though the combination of warm days and cool nights needed to get sap from the maples doesn't always occur, the staff at Bruce's Mill believe the show must go on. To that end they keep a supply of sap to use in demonstrations even when Mother Nature doesn't cooperate.

THE BEST OF SAP ON TAP

A quintessential part of the Canadian spring, an abundance of maple syrup activities take place in Southern Ontario. Because syrup production varies with the weather, it is always wise to phone ahead to

*if you go*

DIRECTIONS: Bruce's Mill is on the south side of the Stouffville Road, 3 km (2 miles) east of Highway 404.

SCHEDULE: Syrup season usually lasts about three weeks, from mid- to late March. During this time Bruce's Mill is open weekdays 9:30 a.m. to 4:30 p.m., weekends 10 a.m. to 5 p.m.

ADMISSION: Adults $2, seniors $1.50, children 5 to 14 $1, children under 5 free.

INFORMATION: Call (416) 661-6600

MAP REFERENCE: 8

## Bruce's Mill Conservation Area Sugar Bush

confirm dates, hours and activities. Most sugar bush activities begin in mid-March and continue into early April. Bruce's Mill is a guaranteed hit, but other good choices include the Kortright Centre for Conservation, near Kleinburg, where both new and pioneer methods are demonstrated along a woodland nature trail.

At Black Creek Pioneer Village there is a modest demonstration of nineteenth-century methods, and ample opportunity to learn how the sweet stuff was used in pioneer cooking to make everything from beer to candy. Both Kortright and Black Creek are administered by the Metropolitan Toronto and Region Conservation Authority; call (416) 661-6600.

A beautiful location high on the Niagara Escarpment makes Hamilton's Royal Botanical Gardens' sugar bush one of the most popular. In the Royal Botanical Gardens' Rock Chapel Sanctuary visitors can tour the modern operation, sample syrup, then hike the scenic south-facing slopes of the escarpment, studded with the first signs of spring: green shoots of garlic mustard and chickadees chirping their mating calls. Trails provide stunning views of the surrounding countryside, distant steel mills and office towers of Hamilton, as well as Lake Ontario. On weekends pancakes are served doused in maple syrup — as long as supplies last. Call (416) 527-7962 for details.

If you want to see the original methods of syrup-making as discovered by Woodland Indians, nothing beats Crawford Lake Conservation Area, near Milton. In a reconstructed Native village staff demonstrate pre-European methods, cutting a V-shaped gash into trees with a stone axe and letting the sap drip into birchbark buckets. Cooked with fire-heated rocks, the syrup is dark and smoky. Call (416) 336-1158 or (416) 854-0234. See page 38 for additional details on Crawford Lake.

## Aquafarms, Feversham

Trout season lasts year-round at Aquafarms, south of Collingwood, but you don't have to be a fisherman to enjoy a visit to the watery farm that raises more than a million trout a year. Knowledgeable staff are on hand to explain how the popular sport fish are bred and raised to a size suitable to grace a dinner plate.

Proprietor Alex Plomp traveled the world with a Swedish colleague setting up fish farms in the United States, Spain, Denmark, Sweden, Norway and Scotland before opening this operation in 1975. His expertise is still sought, particularly by several North American Native bands who are turning to fish farming because of diminishing and polluted wild fish stocks.

Visitors to Plomp's Aquafarms learn about fish farming at its most successful. Autumn is the season when visitors can see the breeding business in action as massive brood trout weighing up to 9 kg (20 pounds) are squeezed to release their eggs and sperm. Breeding, which continues until early January, is not left to the whims of nature. Fast-growing fish are specially selected to live out their days as breeders. Separated into different tanks, males and females are not even brought together at breeding time. Instead, the fish are manipulated by human hands.

Large females, which are typically bigger than males, can be difficult to handle, so to keep fighting fish sedate, an anesthetic is required. The fish is scooped from her pond and eased into a tank containing a sedative that is absorbed through the gills. When the trout rolls over on her side the staff have five minutes, the length of time the fish can stay out of the water, to gently squeeze out the orange eggs. Males are then "milked" of their sperm, which must be poured over the tray of eggs within three minutes of the eggs leaving the female's body. In four months the fertilized eggs will grow into fingerlings 5 to 7 cm (2 to 3 inches) long.

The ten outdoor ponds remain teeming with trout throughout the winter months, when solar energy is used to heat the water, pumped from the Beaver River, to 12° C (54° F). Lined with heavy blue vinyl, the rectangular ponds resemble wading pools, except for the splashing of leaping

## *Aquafarms*

trout. The vinyl helps to protect tender trout fins that might be scraped on a cement bottom. A dirty bottom can make fish taste muddy, so a vacuum pump cleans the water of solid waste, which is then used as fertilizer.

The peaceful sounds of babbling water and splashing trout are interrupted every fifteen minutes when explosive blasts leave startled visitors looking around for the smoking gun. They are soon reassured that nothing's wrong; it's just the feeders going off. Pellets made of mackerel meal, soya and salmon oil are released into the tanks at regular intervals.

Most visitors are surprised to learn of the efficiency with which the trout absorb their food. The farm uses 1 kg (2.2 pounds) of fish food to produce 1 kg of trout, and the farm's rainbow trout are estimated to grow at least twice as fast as the wild speckled trout in the river. The controlled breeding at the farm is also remarkably efficient; 95 percent of the fish eggs develop into mature fish at the farm, compared to 1 percent in the wild.

Visitors wishing to buy trout may catch their own in a well-stocked pond surrounded by grassy banks and picnic tables, or simply have one scooped out of a tank. A gift shop boasts a display of trout-raising equipment; it also sells smoked trout and boneless fillets ready for the pan. During winter it is not unusual to see cross-country skiers striding through the snow on their way back from Aquafarms with a bag of fresh trout. The fish's succulent, rosy flesh makes the trip worthwhile.

### *if you go*

**DIRECTIONS:** Aquafarms is north of Feversham on the 12th Concession. From Highway 24 turn west at Highway 4, then follow the signs. Feversham is roughly 120 km (75 miles) northwest of Metro Toronto, via Highways 10 and 24.

**SCHEDULE:** Open daily 8 a.m. to 6 p.m. during the summer, 9 a.m. to 5 p.m. during the winter.

**ADMISSION:** Free. Live salmon trout are sold for $4.50 a pound, rainbow trout for $4 a pound.

**INFORMATION:** Call (519) 922-2817

**MAP REFERENCE:** 19

## scenic waterways

## R.M.S. Segwun, *Gravenhurst*

Even though the age of steam has long passed, there is no shortage of folks who crave the romance of an era when any long-distance travel invariably took place on steam trains and steamer ships.

Today the steam whistle is heard again, summoning passengers to the Gravenhurst dock where the last passenger steamship in the Muskoka lakes is restored and running once again. Steamers like the Royal Mail Steamship *Segwun* were once a common sight on waterways all over Canada, but today the *Segwun* is a rare bird. With more than a century behind her she is one of the oldest steam-driven ships on this side of the Atlantic and one of the few iron-hulled vessels left in the world.

Long before the railroad was built, the Muskoka lakes steamers were ferrying mail, passengers and supplies across wilderness waterways. Today the *Segwun* ferries steamship enthusiasts and vacationers on a variety of cruises ranging in length from ninety minutes to nine hours. If you have a day to spend in Muskoka, the Lake Rosseau Cruise "in the genuine, authentic steamboat tradition" is perhaps the most pleasant way you might ever find to while away seven and a half hours. The leisurely cruise takes passengers north across Lake Muskoka, through the lock at Port Carling and into Lake Rosseau, where passengers are dropped off at one of the grand old Muskoka resorts, usually Windermere, for lunch.

Seen through the early-morning mists, the *Segwun* at dock takes an onlooker by surprise. A historic plaque beside the road informs passengers that the last of the Muskoka steamers went out of service in 1958. It's enough to make one wonder if this old ship is real. But get up close and any doubt is dispelled.

With a blast of its whistle, the *Segwun* departs from the Gravenhurst dock. There is surprisingly little noise. Outboard motorboats that roar past throughout the day seem like noisy nuisances compared with the graceful tranquillity of the *Segwun*'s dual-cylinder engines.

Within a few minutes on the lake it becomes clear that this is not just a sightseeing cruise; it's also a historical voyage. From the bridge the captain comments on the scenic highlights and talks about travel on the Muskoka steamers of old.

As the *Segwun* nears Millionaire's Row, near Beaumaris, visitors hear how Gravenhurst, a lumber town in the 1880s, made the transition to tourism when the railways advertised the virtues of Canada's lakes and forests to wealthy American sportsmen. There was so much traffic, in fact, that the four Royal Mail steamers of the day would pull alongside one another on Lake Muskoka and put out adjoining gangplanks so mail and passengers could be moved from ship to ship without the bother of docking.

The *Segwun* was not the grandest of the steamers — she was outclassed by the fleet flagship, *Sagamo* — but today her old-fashioned looks are elegant. Victorian-style park benches grace the outer decks, and brass in the engine room is polished to a bright gleam. Passengers may sip a gin and tonic in the oak-paneled lounge and feel as though they belong to a more elegant era. The restorers have paid careful attention to detail, keeping the old fire-fighting buckets and lifeboats in sight while installing modern safety equipment. Even the old mailbox has been kept; post a letter there and it will be franked "R.M.S. *Segwun*."

Meals, usually lunch and dinner, are served in a gracious dining room on the lower deck. Paneled with pale South American gumwood, the room is a Victorian delight of white tablecloths, fresh flowers and lots of

> *if you go*
>
> DIRECTIONS: The *Segwun* sails from the Gravenhurst dock. From Highway 400 take Highway 169 into the town of Gravenhurst to the dock. The dock is marked clearly.
>
> SCHEDULE: Daily early June to early October.
>
> FARES: Prices for the *Segwun* cruises range from about $12 (for ninety minutes) to $45.95 for the nine-hour cruise (includes a two-hour lunch stop), for adults. Children's prices range from $6 to $34.95. Meals cost extra.
>
> INFORMATION: Cruises may be booked through the Muskoka Lakes Navigation and Hotel Co. Ltd., (705) 687-6667, or through The Cruise People in Toronto, telephone (416) 759-7772. Reservations for meals should be made at the time of booking.
>
> MAP REFERENCE: 10

## *R.M.S.* Segwun

windows providing a full view of the lake. The ship takes ninety passengers while the dining room seats only twenty-eight, so reservations are necessary when booking a cruise.

Wherever she sails, the *Segwun* attracts a crowd. Cottagers and campers come down to the docks to wave to the ship. Children ask the captain to blow the whistle. At Port Carling traffic backs up as far as the eye can see, and it seems as though everyone in town has turned out to watch her pass under the drawbridge and through the lock. To cruise on the *Segwun* is to be part of an event.

## Lift Lock, Peterborough

As a commercial venture, the Trent-Severn Waterway could only be classed as an idea whose time had come and gone before it ever opened. Built in the late nineteenth century, the series of canals and locks linking lakes and rivers all the way from Georgian Bay to Lake Ontario was envisioned as a means of transporting grain and logs from the hinterland to the heartland. But its importance as a transportation network soon dwindled when faced with competition from the Welland Canal and newly built railroads.

The commercial flop of the nineteenth century, however, became a twentieth-century tourism success. Today the waterway has become the preserve of pleasure boaters who cruise its 400 km (250 miles) in pursuit of nothing more serious than fish, fun and a good place to swim. But the truth is, you don't even need a boat to enjoy the Trent-Severn Waterway, since it winds through many scenic towns accessible by car.

Fenelon Falls, Bobcaygeon, Buckhorn and Lakefield are among the settlements along the watery route where motorists can watch the marine traffic. Perhaps the best place to understand the magnitude of the waterway is the city of Peterborough, where one of the Trent-Severn's most impressive locks is situated.

When the Hydraulic Lift Lock was opened in 1904 it was celebrated as an engineering first. In fact, it wouldn't be far wrong to compare the magnitude of the project to building the SkyDome or the CN Tower. It was the world's highest lift lock and the largest unreinforced concrete structure. Looming like a fortress gate over the waterway, the Hydraulic Lift Lock raises boats in a single step. This giant lift provided a great shortcut, replacing several smaller locks and enabling commercial traffic to move swiftly through the system.

Today it remains an endless source of fascination for visitors who wait along the grassy banks to see it in action. Unlike conventional locks, which raise boats by flooding, the lift lock lifts containers full of water and bobbing boats like a bathtub full of toy craft. Boats ranging from canoes to cabin cruisers are elevated 30 m (100 feet) in 90 seconds,

## Lift Lock

compared to the conventional lock's 3.5 m (12 feet) in 12 minutes.

The sight of boats being hoisted high above the Kawartha countryside is bound to inspire curiosity, so the Canadian Parks Service (which now administers the entire Trent-Severn Waterway) has wisely selected this spot as the site for an interpretive centre.

In air-conditioned comfort, visitors can pore over an impressive collection of historic photographs depicting the difficulties in the canal's construction. Muddy ditches that look as bleak as First World War trenches and horse-drawn wagons loaded with stone and planks awash in a flooded construction site are testimony to the setbacks that made this Canada's longest-running public works project. Construction began in 1833 and finished in 1920.

Staff are on hand to answer questions. Attractive videos show the waterway in all seasons. Working models of the waterway clearly illustrate its complex operation. There are even sound effects of chugging engines to enliven the display of the utility steam boiler and other construction equipment.

Outside, the tree-shaded lawns make a pleasant picnic spot to watch activity on the waterway, and tables are thoughtfully situated so landlubbers can watch canal traffic while enjoying lunch on the grassy banks.

To experience the lift lock firsthand, you can take one of the Lift Lock Cruises that depart from the marina on the south side of the Holiday Inn on George St. The two-hour trip features an entertaining commentary pointing out sights along the route and recounting the history of the canal. Only when the cruise has passed through the lock does the commentator describe two horrific, but not fatal, boating accidents on the lift lock. Apparently the bathtublike chamber broke open, and in one case, the boats were sucked out with the emptying water. The fault has since been found, nervous cruisers are assured, and preventive measures have been taken.

Explorations of the waterway can comfortably be continued at the

Old Bridge Inn at Young's Point. The inn, a folksy red-brick building that dates back to 1870, takes its name from a century-old footbridge now restored. Visitors can walk to the nearby lock, or just laze about on the banks watching boats buzz by. Four of the eight guest rooms face the water, affording occupants not only a view but also the gentle sounds of gurgling water to lull them to sleep. The inn has an attractive dining room of polished wood and gleaming brass.

### *if you go*

DIRECTIONS: From Highway 401 take Highway 115 north into Peterborough. The Peterborough Lift Lock and the Canadian Parks Service visitors' centre is on Hunter St. E. in Peterborough. Follow the Parks Service beaver signs.

SCHEDULE: Open year-round. Victoria Day to Labour Day, daily 9 a.m. to 6 p.m. Other seasons, Wednesday to Sunday 10 a.m. to 5 p.m. Winter skating on the canal from 10 a.m. to 10 p.m.

ADMISSION: Free. Parking and washrooms are provided.

INFORMATION: Call (705) 742-2251

ACCOMMODATION: Rates at the Old Bridge Inn (South Beach Rd., Youngs Point, K0L 3G0) are $60 double, including continental breakfast. The dining room is open from Mother's Day to Thanksgiving, but the inn's guest rooms are open year-round. Call (705) 652-8507 for details. Visa, MasterCard.

The Lift Lock Cruises run from mid-June to September. They depart at 11 a.m., 1:30 and 4 p.m. The latter two are one-way trips that include a return trip by sightseeing bus. For adults the price is $14, children $7. Call (705) 742-9912.

MAP REFERENCE: 4

# Maid of the Mist, *Niagara Falls*

For more than a century Niagara Falls has been a hit with tourists from around the world. The camera-clicking hordes are drawn by the natural spectacle of the falls, but once they get here they find another sort of spectacle: an eyeful of wax museum monsters, daredevil paraphernalia and other commercial gimmicks. Few of these so-called attractions fit in with Ma Nature's stately grandeur: most make a hefty dent in the wallet. That's why the *Maid of the Mist* is so special. The tiny flotilla of *Maid* tour boats that carry passengers to the foot of the thundering falls is one of the few attractions that really complement the natural wonder.

Dwarfed by the falls, the four boats plying the waters of the lower Niagara River seem like mere toys when seen from lookouts high above the gorge. In fact they are substantial craft, with long histories dating back well over a century.

As early as 1843, many small craft were taking passengers across the river, but tourists were nervous about negotiating the turbulent currents in tiny rowboats. In 1846 the Niagara Falls Ferry Association began a sidewheeler steamboat ferry service that carried passengers, baggage, mail and freight between the U.S. and Canada. That boat, the first *Maid of the Mist*, took her name from a Native legend about a beautiful maiden who was sent over the falls in a canoe as a sacrifice because members of her tribe were dying for unknown reasons.

With the advent of a suspension bridge spanning the river in 1848, the steamboat was no longer necessary for basic transportation. However, tourism continued to be a booming business, so the owners began using the *Maid* for pleasure trips to the foot of the falls.

That tradition continues today, and each ship in the flotilla carries as many as 300 passengers on twenty-minute trips to the foot of the falls. Passengers ride a funicular railway to the bottom of the gorge, where they don ankle-length raincoats. On a sunny spring afternoon, when a rainbow is forming above the mist, the coats with their large hoods may seem like overkill. However, once the boat passes the foot of the

American Falls and heads for the Horseshoe Falls, the mist becomes a shower. Tourists are soon rolling up their trouser legs to save them from the deluge on deck.

The *Maid*s pause at the foot of the thundering Horseshoe Falls for about five minutes — long enough for everyone to get wet shoes, wet hair and a face full of spray — before turning back to the dock. The spray is so thick that it obscures the view even on a sunny day. Spring is the best time of year to see the panorama, before the humidity of summer creates a haze.

Despite the savage currents, the *Maid*s have never lost a passenger, but they have seen a few adventures. Back in 1861, when the second *Maid of the Mist* was sold to a Montreal firm, it had to be delivered through Lake Ontario. Even river pilots who regularly braved the Long Sault and Lachine Rapids in the St. Lawrence refused to sail her down the dangerous Niagara River. Finally, *Maid of the Mist*'s Captain Robinson agreed to do the job.

Two men gripped the wheel, but the force of rushing water from both sides of the river turned the *Maid* on her side and ripped off the smokestack. Captain Robinson, who was thrown to the deck, managed to regain control as the *Maid* was tossed through the whirlpool and shot into the rapids. After Robinson delivered her to Queenston, he refused to negotiate the Niagara River for the rest of his life.

The boats currently sailing in the gorge are named *Maid of the Mist I, III, IV* and *V*. Number I is not the original, but a 1955 boat built after a fire destroyed two of the old oak ships. When the newest *Maid* began operating in 1983, the Number II boat was refitted to serve as a missionary ship plying the Amazon.

Another popular way to get a close-up view of the falls is by helicopter. If your budget permits this more pricey thrill, Niagara Helicopters Ltd. is recommended for its exciting sightseeing flight on board rainbow-striped turbine choppers. Taking off from a launch pad near the Niagara Parks Commission's School of Horticulture, the

## Maid of the Mist

helicopters buzz over the whirlpool rapids and the Rainbow Bridge en route to the Horseshoe Falls, where they give passengers some eye-popping, heart-stopping thrills by flying two full-circle loops over the falls. The view is spectacular along the Niagara Gorge with its massive powerplants, the tree-lined parkway, the city stretching out in the distance, and most impressive of all — the falls.

Niagara Helicopters uses two four-seater Jet Rangers, a Bell six-seater Long Ranger, and a whopping Bell 412 fourteen-seater, like the kind used for offshore flights to oil rigs. Most days the six-seater ferries a nonstop parade of passengers.

It all happens so quickly — eight minutes from takeoff to landing — that there barely seems time to digest the view. But even after the rushed disembarkation of almost military precision, the thrill does linger.

### *if you go*

**THE MAID OF THE MIST**

**DIRECTIONS:** *The Maid of the Mist*, 5920 River Rd., at the foot of Clifton Hill in Niagara Falls. Boats depart from the dock, just downstream from the falls. Boats also sail from the U.S. side.

**SCHEDULE:** The season usually begins in mid-May and continues until late October. Boats depart every 15 minutes during peak periods, every 30 minutes at other times.

**COST:** The boat trip costs $7.75 for adults, $4.40 for children 6 to 12. There is also a $1 charge for the incline railway trip for those who don't want to walk up and down the stairs to the dock.

**INFORMATION:** Call (416) 358-5781

**MAP REFERENCE:** 13

**NIAGARA HELICOPTERS**

**DIRECTIONS:** Niagara Helicopters is on the east side of the Niagara Parkway at 3731 Victoria Ave. From Niagara Falls drive north to Victoria Ave., near the Whirlpool Rapids.

**SCHEDULE:** Niagara Helicopters flies from 9 a.m. to dusk, seven days a week.

**COST:** Rates are $61 per person, $107 per couple, $15 per child.

**INFORMATION:** Call (416) 357-5672

**MAP REFERENCE:** 13

# The Port Dover Harbour Museum, Port Dover

With gulls hanging on the breeze above the harbour and fishing boats unloading their catch at the dock, it looks for all the world like an Atlantic fishing village, but the dock is situated in Port Dover, one of the fishing towns that make the Lake Erie shoreline perfect for anyone who craves a maritime flavour.

During the summer months Port Dover is a riot of go-karts and french fries, but in the spring and fall visitors see it for what it really is — one of the largest freshwater fishing ports in North America.

About three dozen commercial fishing boats bring in catches of smelt, perch, pickerel and bass. Other folk may prize salmon and sole, but the fillet most Port Dover people prefer on their plates is a freshwater variety of perch that abounds in Lake Erie. Many of the fishing boats operate well into the winter, and fresh perch can be bought at wharfside fish markets. A trip to Port Dover isn't complete without a stop at Knetchels, the fast-food outlet that specializes in fried perch and chips, a humble but honorable culinary classic.

To learn more about Port Dover's maritime heritage, explore the Port Dover Harbour Museum, a former net shanty now containing more than 200 artifacts from Lake Erie's fishing industry. Although the riverside shanty is small, it's a fascinating place, crammed full of information about the interesting but little-known history of the area. Visitors should be sure to talk to curator Sylvia Crossland, who will tell stories of icebound rescues on the lake and some of the numerous shipwrecks that have occurred off Long Point in the past two centuries. A sandy spit that juts 30 km (19 miles) into Lake Erie, Long Point presented a hazard to schooners seeking the shelter of the inner harbour during a gale. In the early half of the nineteenth-century, other schooners were lured onto the banks by pirates using misleading safety lights.

If the museum whets your appetite for a boat trip, you may be able to arrange an hour-long cruise on the *Peggy Jane*, an open tour boat that sails from the dock in front of the museum, if it can get at least eight passengers. It travels up and down the river (Black Creek), past the

## The Port Dover Harbour Museum

industrial shipyards, then into Lake Erie. If you want to take a cruise, make arrangements at the museum.

A great little bed-and-breakfast for a weekend base is the Union Hotel, in the nearby village of Normandale. Once a busy commercial hostelry, the hotel is now a charming country inn. The sleepy village of Normandale was the site of Upper Canada's first iron foundry. Built in 1818 when John Mason discovered the local bog ore, Normandale's furnace prospered and died before Canada ever became a nation.

During its heyday, though, Americans sailed across Lake Erie and tinkers journeyed from across Upper Canada to buy supplies of posts, hinges, nails and even cook stoves manufactured at the foundry. So numerous were visitors that Normandale businessmen decided the town needed accommodation. They banded together to build the Union Hotel.

The Normandale Furnaces produced their last door hinge long ago, but the guests are still coming to the restored hotel. The Peets bought the rundown frame building in 1971 and did an admirable job of restoring it. There may be nothing more than a babbling brook and a historical plaque where the foundry used to be, but visitors can still see some of its goods at the hotel. The Norfolk-style latches on the doors were made at the foundry.

During summer people come to

---

**if you go**

DIRECTIONS: To reach Port Dover, take Highway 6 south from Hamilton. The Port Dover Harbour Museum is at 44 Harbour St., on Black Creek, near the Lift Bridge.

SCHEDULE: The museum is open daily from mid-May to Labour Day from 10 a.m. to 6 p.m.; weekends to Thanksgiving.

ADMISSION: Free, but donations are appreciated.

INFORMATION: Call (519) 583-2660. You may also call this number to arrange a boat trip on the *Peggy Jane* (minimum eight people needed), at $6 per person.

ACCOMMODATION: The Union Hotel, Box 38, R.R. 1, Normandale, NOE 1W0. The hotel is approximately 15 km (9 miles) west of Port Dover. It charges $50 a night double, including full breakfast. Call (519) 426-5568. No credit cards.

MAP REFERENCE: 14

the north shore of Erie for the sandy beaches (Turkey Point Provincial Park in particular). In spring bird-watching is excellent. Autumn is the season to enjoy walking the trails (which turn to ski routes in the winter). Stretching from the Union Hotel's front door are a good 8 km (5 miles) of woodland paths.

After an outing guests warm their hands over a wood-burning stove in the Union's cosy dining room. It seats only twenty and has no liquor licence, but its candlelight dinners and good home cooking have made it very popular, especially on weekends.

There are only three guest rooms, and they share a washroom at the end of the hall. But bedrooms boast such folksy touches as country antiques, handmade rag rugs, quilts and hand-embroidered cotton pillowcases.

# Welland Canal Lock N°3 Viewing Complex, St. Catharines

Seafaring fantasies are sometimes difficult to indulge in an inland province, but the Welland Canal is a great place to live out a stowaway's daydream. From the observation platform at St. Catharines, you can watch the progress of behemoth freighters full of grain and iron ore slogging along the eight-lock canal from Lake Ontario to Lake Erie.

Built to bypass Ontario's biggest tourist attraction, Niagara Falls, the Welland Canal has become a tourist attraction itself, with museums devoted to exploring its past and parks for watching the ships' progress.

The highlight of the canal system is the Welland Canal Viewing and Information Centre and Museum at Lock 3, St. Catharines. This year-round modern complex features videos and displays on the canal, a covered viewing platform, a restaurant, a gift shop and the relocated St. Catharines Historical Museum. Among the museum's spiffy new displays are a massive computerized working model of Lock No. 3, built to scale, as well as an original 1912 REO car, the forerunner of the Oldsmobile, built in St. Catharines.

Visitors can buy a snack to eat at the patio or take advantage of picnic facilities along the banks of the canal. Relax over your meal and watch the freighters laden with ore and grain moving through the massive twin lock. Listed on a markerboard are the upbound and downbound arrival times along with details such as each ship's size, cargo, nationality and destination. Exotic names are not unusual; roughly half of the traffic on the canal is made up of oceangoing vessels. Every year these massive ships carry nearly 40 million tonnes of raw materials out of the country's heartland to distant corners of the earth.

Ship-watching is not a pastime for the impatient. There can be a five-hour wait between scheduled arrivals; when the ships finally do come they move as slowly as overloaded tortoises, trying to manoeuvre their great bulk into long, narrow locks with barely a foot to spare on each side. To help pass the time while waiting, and to put the canal into a broader perspective, visitors can watch an eight-minute film in the

Burgoyne Room that shows how the canal functions as part of the St. Lawrence Seaway System.

If the wait looks as if it is going to be a long one, it is well worth heading for Port Dalhousie, known locally as "Port Daloosie." Follow tree-lined Government St. north to Lock No. 1, where you can watch the shipbuilding at the Port Weller Dry Docks. Then turn west onto Lakeshore Rd., which will take you to the old town that was the original harbour for the first three Welland canals.

More than a watery highway for ships, the canal has always been an important source of revenue to the communities that sprang up along its banks to supply goods and services for ships and sailors. The original canal emptied into Port Dalhousie, leading to its development into a prosperous shipping town. When the canal was straightened and moved about 8 km (5 miles) away, the town dwindled into a sleepy suburb of St. Catharines.

The red-brick warehouses that once held stores of hardtack biscuits, salted meat, rigging and lines were left to decay until renovation fever hit town about a decade ago. Today, the wonderful old waterfront buildings have been converted to boutiques and restaurants. Sections of the old canal with stone locks and wooden gates have been restored. In the days of

---

*if you go*

**DIRECTIONS:** From the Queen Elizabeth Way take Highway 406 at St. Catharines to Glendale Ave. and follow the blue-and-white signs to reach Lock No. 3 and the Viewing Complex and museum.

**SCHEDULE:** The Viewing Complex is open daily year-round. May to Labour Day 9 a.m. to 9 p.m., early September to late April 9 a.m. to 5 p.m.

**ADMISSION:** The Viewing Complex is free. Museum rates: adults $3, youths and seniors $2, elementary school students $1, family $7.

**INFORMATION:** Viewing Complex ship report, (416) 685-3711. Museum, (416) 984-8880.

Port Dalhousie: The carousel is open afternoons daily mid-June to Labour Day. Weekends only, mid-May to mid-June, weather permitting. Hours of operation are noon to 8 p.m. (with a closing from 4:30 to 5:15 p.m.). For more information call the St. Catharines Parks and Recreation Dept. at (416) 937-7210.

**MAP REFERENCE:** 13

## Welland Canal Lock N°3 Viewing Complex

bloomers and bonnets, summer steamers used to bring shiploads of tourists from Toronto to cool off on Port Dalhousie's beach. Today, the tourists are more likely to sail into port on pleasure craft and moor at the local club.

One wonderful artifact from yesteryear is the carousel at Lakeside Park. Hand-carved and gaily painted chariots, horses, lions and giraffes circle four abreast to calliope music. Unfortunately, an ugly brick building was necessary to protect the carousel from vandals, but when it opens up on summer afternoons visitors can still ride the antique carousel for the antique price of a nickel.

Port Dalhousie is also the site of the Royal Canadian Henley Regatta, held each summer on Martindale Pond, once part of the old Welland Canal system. It is one of the top rowing events in North America and attracts thousands of competitors from around the world. It is usually held the first weekend in August.

## *Historic Naval and Military Establishments, Penetanguishene*

Deck-swabbing sailors soon put visitors to work at the nineteenth-century Naval Establishments. Before long, even the youngest recruit will be caulking a bateau, making ropes and sawing planks in an ambitious hands-on program that makes the Historic Naval and Military Establishments at Penetanguishene a great summer adventure for both children and adults.

The stage is set in the visitors' centre where landlubbers get a summarized history of the site, dating back to 1817 when the British intended to build a strong line of defense along the Great Lakes. An uneasy peace led to the development of the naval base into a supply depot and shipyard. By 1834, Anglo-American relations had thawed, and the Royal Navy left the base to the army, who stayed till 1856.

Today visitors are given a free brochure so they can explore the site at their own pace or wander along dirt footpaths leading to reconstructed buildings where sailors, captains and craftsmen go about their business as though wooden schooners were still being used to ship military supplies to points west.

At Bayfield House you learn of the early 1820 explorations of hydrographer Henry Bayfield, who with his crew accurately charted up to a hundred islands a day in the Great Lakes. From May to December, Bayfield and his men were at work, but during winter months he came back to this house to plot data for future chart work. His work is still used as the basis for many navigational charts.

At the Commanding Officer's House visitors get a sense of the loneliness of the posting. Here Capt. Samuel Roberts lived and worked, sharing the clapboard house with his wife and her sister. Drunkenness was so prevalent that the women rarely ventured outdoors for walks; instead they busied themselves in books and needlework. A cook would have been provided from among the ranks of the sailors, who were often pressed into unusual roles at Penetanguishene. The Georgian Bay post was so isolated that food was very expensive to import, and seamen were

## Historic Naval and Military Establishments

set to work tending vegetable gardens.

On-site mini dramas bring the issues of the day to life, with characters heatedly discussing the difficult travel on corduroy roads as well as the latest London fashions. When the captain calls the guard to dismiss a drunk and disorderly sailor from the base, visitors soon learn the hardships of naval life. Dismissal or desertion often meant death for the sailor sent into the wilderness without compass or supplies. York, the nearest town, was a three-to-five-day walk away.

The sailor's life was certainly hard, the working day long and the pay puny. It was made endurable only by a grog-induced haze that no doubt led to disorderly conduct, hence the need to guard supplies of food and rum. The former naval storehouse, where eighteen months' worth of supplies were stockpiled, including gunpowder, yellow peas and rum rations, has been converted to a summer stock theatre with live productions of shows like *Godspell* or a version of *Billy Budd*.

Down by the dockyard, a shipwright steams planks in a coffin so they can be curved to fit a hull. Another shows visitors how to seal the hull of a bateau with oakum caulking, a mixture of old rope fibers and tar hammered into cracks between planks.

As modern motorboats buzz along the bay, a touch of nineteenth-century nautical realism is provided by the three tall ships moored at the dock: the *Perseverance*, an 83-foot cargo schooner; a 100-foot replica of the British naval schooner the H.M.S. *Tecumseth*; and the *Schooner Bee*, a replica of the 1817 supply ship once stationed here. Like the original that delivered supplies to the Drummond Island post in Georgian Bay, the *Bee* looks wooden right down to her cleats and blocks (but is fiberglass underneath and conforms to modern safety standards). Daytime visitors are welcomed on board, where a young sailor shows them how to swab a deck using sand, which was rubbed onto the wood with a holy stone, then swabbed off with a mop.

To really experience the navy life, though, visitors should sign up for one of the Sailor's Sunset cruises, where they can play at being scurvy sea dogs for an evening. They'll have a tour of the Establishments before being mustered into the Royal Navy by a not-so-gruff sailing master. "The crew will ask you to do jobs, but if you don't do them I won't have you flogged."

But the landlubbers are soon given a few seafaring tips ("the pointy end is the bow") and put to work. The crew are all members of the Ship's Company, a group of volunteers who share a passion for history, sailing and good times. Dressed in the style of 1820s sailors — blue felt jackets and straw hats — they live out their roles right down to the seadog insults. With crew watching every move, visiting sailors work the sheets while tacking across the water, then put their muscles to the test sweeping the vessel into harbour. To landlubbers that means rowing the fifty-foot schooner with six long oars. In addition to the *Schooner Bee* Sailor's Sunset cruises, other instructional cruises are offered.

## if you go

**DIRECTIONS:** The Historic Naval and Military Establishments are in Penetanguishene. From Highway 400 follow Highway 93 into Penetanguishene, and follow the Huronia Heritage signs to the end of Church St.

**SCHEDULE:** Open daily from mid-May to Labour Day. May and June 10 a.m. to 5 p.m., July 1 to Labour Day 10 a.m. to 8 p.m.

**ADMISSION:** Adults $5, seniors $2, students $3, children 6 and under free.

**INFORMATION:** Call Huronia Historical Parks at (705) 526-7838.

**CRUISES:** The three-hour evening sail begins at 5 p.m. Tuesday, Thursday and Saturday during July and August. Each Sailor's Sunset accommodates 12 people. Participants must be 10 years of age and over. The fee is $30. Reserve by contacting Historic Naval and Military Establishments, Box 1800, Penetanguishene, L0K 1P0, telephone (705) 549-8064. Tall ship programs for families and children are also available.

**MAP REFERENCE:** 9

*scenic waterways*

## *Flowerpot Island, Tobermory*

**P**ostcard-perfect harbours, flower-studded hiking trails and an underwater park full of shipwrecks have made Tobermory a mecca for Canadian divers, boaters and nature-lovers. Roughly two dozen sunken ships can be found in the waters of Fathom Five National Marine Park, but it is not necessary to be a diver to see some of these seabound skeletons. Boat tours make them readily accessible, along with the area's scenic attractions, such as the impressive landscape of Flowerpot Island.

Here at the tip of the Bruce Peninsula, the Niagara Escarpment pokes into Georgian Bay like a bony limestone finger. The location creates a sense of isolation that makes the area a natural spot for a quiet retreat. Its harbours draw a parade of pleasure boats and tourists.

People who arrive by car, via Highway 6, can take advantage of the daily summertime boat tours to see the shipwrecks and Flowerpot Island. The M.V. *Seaview III* is one of the most popular boats, offering several departures each day from Little Tub Harbour, weather permitting. A tour typically begins with a jaunt to neighboring Big Tub Harbour to see two wrecks: an 1867 wooden schooner and an 1879 steamer. Although the *Seaview* is equipped with a glass window for an underwater view, the wrecks are so close to the surface — 7 and 5 m (23 and 17 feet) deep, respectively — and the water is so clear that they can easily be seen from the ship's upper deck.

According to the ship's commentary this is the deepest natural freshwater harbour in the world, with depths of 20 m (65 feet). Impressive cottages line the shore, and on a pleasant weekend it is not uncommon to spot divers in wetsuits readying their scuba tanks for a dive to one of the sunken ships. Most cruises will make arrangements to drop passengers for an hour, or a day, on Flowerpot Island, where they can explore roughly 6 km (3 3/4 miles) of hiking trails. It is an experience not to be missed.

On a sunny day the island's rocky shore takes on a Caribbean look: white rocks dropping off to clear, intensely blue waters. Flowerpot takes its name from the odd geological formations that dot its shores. The limestone cliffs of the island, which are part of the Niagara Escarpment, have soft lower strata easily carved by water. Eventually tall sections are cut off from the mainland, standing like chimneys poking above the Georgian Bay waves. With scruffy trees growing from their tops these limestone chimneys look like giant flowerpots.

Flowerpot's limestone cliffs were part of a tropical sea 500 million years ago, and in places the limestone still holds fossils from those early marine animals. A trail leads to a hilltop cave carved by waves when the water levels were higher. The cave roof was once part of an ancient coral reef, and in its ceiling can be seen the shapes of cephalopod fossils, distant ancestors to the modern squid.

A path covered with wood chips makes easy hiking through forested

*if you go*

DIRECTIONS: Tobermory is at the northern tip of the Bruce Peninsula. Travel north on Highway 6. Cruises depart from Little Tub Harbour in the main part of town.

SCHEDULE: The *Seaview* sails from May to mid-October, six cruises daily during the peak months, starting at 9 a.m. Cruises last 90 minutes.

ADMISSION: Fares are $11 for adults, $7 for children. There is a 50-cent surcharge for being dropped off at the island.

INFORMATION: Call the *Seaview*'s proprietor at (519) 596-2950. Or call the Tobermory Lodge below.

ACCOMMODATION: The Grandview Motel, Earl St., telephone (519) 596-2220, charges about $45 double.

The Tobermory Lodge, Box 190, Tobermory, telephone (519) 596-2224, charges $60 to $80 double, cottages $95 to $110. Visa, MasterCard, Amex, Diners Club.

For schedule, rates and reservations on the Chi-Cheemaun ferry contact Ontario Northland in Owen Sound, (519) 376-6601.

For more information on Fathom Five National Marine Park, contact Box 189, Tobermory, NOH 2R0, telephone (519) 596-2233.

MAP REFERENCE: 20

# Flowerpot Island

areas. Warm days bring out dozens of garter snakes that scatter at the sound of footsteps. Few natural predators cross the ice from the mainland to Flowerpot, so the reptiles thrive in peace and are harmless to hikers. The rocky shoreline makes an ideal nesting area for snakes. During spring, the island is a popular spot with orchid hunters, but flowers continue into the autumn with daisies and little orange trumpets of touch-me-nots along the trails.

There are no concessions on the island, so if you plan to spend the day, it's a good idea to pack a picnic — supplies are available in Tobermory. Half a dozen primitive campsites are available on a first-come, first-served basis (for $6 a night) and there are barbecue pits if you plan a cookout. To see some of the artifacts gathered from wrecks, drop in at the Fathom Five Park Office in Tobermory.

The Chi-Cheemaun ferry, which takes up to 140 cars and 600 passengers to Manitoulin Island on its two-hour trips, sails from Tobermory several times a day from late April to mid-October.

A cheap and cheerful motel is The Grandview on Earl St. The rooms are basic but clean, and the dining room is a real treat. It's a pretty room with picture windows overlooking the harbour. Homemade soups, fresh whitefish and good steaks are on the menu. The slightly more expensive Tobermory Lodge is another good choice.

*classic collections*

## Ontario Electric Railway Museum, Guelph

Riding a woodland track past maples, daisies and even the occasional deer, streetcars retired from Toronto's traffic-clogged streets (among other places) have found a new life at the Ontario Electric Railway Museum near Guelph. What makes this museum special is that many of the vehicles in its constantly growing collection of electric railway cars are still in operation, although the passengers are now pleasure riders instead of commuters on their way to work.

Museum visitors climb aboard restored streetcars to ride a 1.5-km (1-mile) stretch of track that was once part of a 1917 electric railway connecting Toronto and Guelph. The ride took two and a half hours and made 100 stops.

Old signs admonishing passengers "No talking to the motorman" are happily ignored by the volunteer crew, who enjoy explaining the history and workings of these efficient old cars. Ringing the bell to startle a squirrel off the track, a volunteer driver explains how car number 2786 put in four dutiful decades of service along Roncesvalles and Dundas in Toronto before retirement in 1963. An advertisement for the long-dead *Telegram* newspaper still shouts its message from the front of the car, part of the detailing that makes these old cars such a perfect trip through time.

Polished wood and brass controls remain little changed today. An air gauge monitors pressure for the brakes, and the motorman uses a handle called the controller to adjust the flow of power, thereby controlling the speed.

Wooden benches and woven straw seats are part of the beautifully restored interior on number 55, built in 1915 for the Toronto Civic Railways, a predecessor of the TTC. Flip passenger seats meant every passenger could face the front when the car reversed at the end of the track. Its lovely interior belies an ignominious second career as a work car. Withdrawn from passenger service in 1926, number 55 was reincarnated as a snow scraper before its retirement.

Multiple reincarnations seem to be common with these well-used vehicles. Among the rusting car skeletons brought in for restoration are streetcars that were built into houses and another that served as a swimming pool change room. Volunteer workers toil away at meticulous restorations, accurate right down to the period paint jobs.

Open cars were among the earliest to trundle through Toronto streets. Modeled after the open cars used in Hogtown during the late 1890s, number 327 offers an alfresco ride on its wooden benches. While intercity trains were equipped with cow catchers, this 1893 model has a net in front dubbed the "pedestrian shoveler." Passengers clambered onto running boards along the sides of the car and held on for a high-speed ride through 15 m.p.h. traffic that eventually was the open car's demise. Deemed unsafe at such speeds, the open cars were withdrawn from city streets.

Not all the old electric cars were pokey vehicles. In 1915 the London & Port Stanley Railway ordered five cars as part of an experiment in high-speed railways. Car number 8 was part of that order and was built to run at up to 85 m.p.h.

Not all of the cars are that old, either. Many people will have recently ridden Toronto's Red Rockets, the affectionate name for the PCC 4000 that revolutionized public transit with safe, sturdy, comfortable cars that put in many years of service.

Visitors can see about two dozen cars that have been restored at the museum, as well as working equipment like rail grinders, buses, trucks and assorted other machinery. Usually three or four favourite cars are put into service on operating days for the public to ride. Special

*if you go*

DIRECTIONS: The Ontario Electric Railway Museum is east of Guelph. From Highway 401 exit at the Guelph Line and drive 15 km (9 miles) north.

SCHEDULE: Open mid-May to late October on weekends and holidays 10 a.m. to 5 p.m. June Wednesday to Sunday. July and August daily.

ADMISSION: Adults $4.75, students $4, seniors and children $2.75. Includes rides.

INFORMATION: Call (519) 856-9802

MAP REFERENCE: 11

## Ontario Electric Railway Museum

Extravaganza days are held in mid-June, late September and late December, when as many as a dozen cars run on the scenic little line.

## Niagara Apothecary Museum, Niagara-on-the-Lake

Gilded monuments and exquisite artworks may be priceless treasures, but the humble objects of day-to-day life are often more curious. It is the familiarity of the drugstore, its remedies and potions, that makes the Niagara Apothecary such a wonderful museum. This is not a building designed to house rare and costly artifacts, but an ordinary nineteenth-century Niagara-on-the-Lake drugstore that has managed to survive into the twentieth century relatively intact.

With only six pharmacist-owners since 1819 (and all but one of them professional descendants through the apprenticeship system), the pharmacy remained in business until the 1960s. Then, after careful restoration, the building reopened as a museum in 1971.

Since then, more than half a million people have passed through its doors to study the antique bottles of patent medicines and admire the craftsmanship of its interior. Any visitor who steps inside is impressed by the authenticity of the details. Not only do the original glass and ceramic apothecary jars still line the walls but the place even smells as one imagines an old drugstore should — having an odor reminiscent of toothpaste, bunion plasters and botanical remedies.

The white clapboard building is an attractive store, reflecting an immense pride of ownership. Serving counters are made of solid black walnut planks nearly half a meter (1 1/2 feet) wide. Crystal chandeliers, reproductions of the originals, hang from plaster medallions on the ceiling, while an ornately carved dispensary bearing a clock dated 1867 dominates the rear of the building.

Down one wall are glass cases filled with fascinating drugstore paraphernalia. Shelves are stacked with antique jars, glass and apothecary ware, as well as hundreds of boxes and bottles of medicines and tonics. Authentic packets of Kellogg Eye Water, Dr. Pierce's Smart-Weed Water Pepper and Hirst's Pectoral Syrup are as interesting as the ornate decor. Many labels shamelessly tout cure-alls for a long list of ailments, like Hamlin's Wizard Oil, which, taken internally or externally,

*classic collections*

## Niagara Apothecary Museum

purportedly cured rheumatism, toothaches, cholera, indigestion and a host of other ailments.

Packaging, then as now, was clearly as important as the ingredients, but one has to wonder about the reasoning that led to selling Suffolk Bitters Life Preserver in a green pig-shaped bottle. Merchant's Gargling Oil might have been better sold that way: the product was billed as "a linament for man and beast."

Medicines were often meant to provide a general feeling of happiness as well as a cure, so Kickapoo Sagwa laxative blithely advertised its 9.5 percent alcohol content. The efficacy of Chamberlain's Colic and Diarrhea Remedy was no doubt aided by its 45 percent alcohol content, and what temperance advocate could object to a tonic used for medicinal purposes?

Tonics abounded for a variety of vague brain, nerve and blood disorders, and their makers advertised their products creatively. Makers of the Great Shosonees Remedy took advantage of the Native-sounding name to suggest a connection with Native remedies, the implication being that indigenous cures would be effective against indigenous ailments.

Museum displays are simple, accompanied only by tidy, typed cards briefly describing the druggists' work. Nineteenth-century apothecaries often sold, in addition to pills, powders and ointments, such household items as curry powder mixed to taste, carbonated beer, waterproof dressing for shoes and tooth powder.

Some of the tools of the ancient trade are on display, including the Niagara Apothecary's well-worn original mortar and pestle, a pill tile and spatula, and a percolator, an 1833 French invention for obtaining botanical extracts. Particularly interesting is a display on pill-making, which was a surprisingly complex business, beginning with the mixing of powders and excipients (binders, such as liquid glucose) in a mortar. The mixture was rolled into a cylindrical pill pipe, then cut on a pill machine. Each piece was rounded by rolling in a boxwood container, then coated and polished. Coatings as varied as varnish, sugar and even precious metals added a great deal of esthetic appeal but often interfered with the action of the medicine.

A drugstore attendant welcomes questions and happily demonstrates the accuracy of the apothecary's original French scales, which can measure the weight of a small paper scrap. An enameled container with air holes once held leeches, and visitors always seem fascinated to hear of the old-fashioned medical uses of these creatures.

In keeping with the spirit of the old drugstore, the Niagara Apothecary still sells a few old-time favourites, like Florida Water, bayberry soap and real licorice root to chew on.

> *if you go*
>
> **DIRECTIONS:** The Niagara Apothecary Museum is in Niagara-on-the-Lake at the corner of Queen and King streets. From Niagara Falls follow the Niagara Parkway north to Queen St.
>
> **SCHEDULE:** Open daily from mid-May to Labour Day, noon to 6 p.m.
>
> **ADMISSION:** Free, but donations are appreciated.
>
> **INFORMATION:** Contact the Ontario College of Pharmacists in Toronto at (416) 962-4861.
>
> **MAP REFERENCE:** 13

## *Canadian Warplane Heritage Museum, Hamilton*

Big-band music wafts through the hangar, and mechanics buzz over vintage aircraft. Visitors strolling past the Dakota and the Chipmunk aircraft could easily imagine they were back in the early 1940s, and this artfully evoked nostalgia is a good indicator of how successful the Canadian Warplane Heritage Museum near Hamilton has become. This is not an ordinary collection. Its forty warbirds (visitors soon learn this is the lingo for warplanes) are refurbished with the intention of being flown, not just of lying parked in a glitzy museum.

Housed in Hangars 3 and 4 at Hamilton Airport, the museum is anything but glitzy. The hangars, built as part of a Second World War training base, make an appropriate home for these active warbirds, all of which have been lovingly restored by volunteers. What began as a private collection in the early 1970s has grown into a full-fledged museum, which now includes a large reference library and a theatre.

Several restoration projects are under way, including a Fairy Firefly and a Hawker Hurricane that survived the Battle of Britain (as well as the movie of the same name). The giant Avro Lancaster was the object of the largest aircraft restoration project in the world. It is not unusual to find this famous heavy bomber parked on the tarmac outside the hangar, being readied for a flight, since it tours Canada attending airshows. Visitors may peer up at the open bomb bays, which once dumped massive payloads over Europe, and imagine the roar of the Lancaster's four Merlin engines as it joined huge formations flying bombing raids over Germany.

The Lancaster has been painted with the wartime markings of the RCAF Moose Squadron No. 419 to commemorate gunner Andrew Mynarski, who earned a Victoria Cross for his attempts to save a fellow gunner trapped in the tail gun section when the plane was hit. Both gunners died, but the rest of the crew survived and have been known to visit the museum.

You don't have to be a former serviceman to reminisce about these aircraft. Many local folk will remember planes from the "canary air force," that fleet of bright yellow aircraft used to train pilots from around the Commonwealth. Flags from those nations are draped from the hangar rafters, including one unusual insignia of triangles, which some people don't immediately recognize. It belongs to Newfoundland, not a member of Confederation until four years after the war.

One thinks of biplanes as belonging to the First World War dogfights of the Red Baron and Billy Bishop, so it comes as a surprise to see them alongside Second World War craft. But the canary yellow Tiger Moth was a popular biplane during the Second World War as a primary trainer, with the instructor flying in the rear. Also on display is the Chipmunk monoplane, which replaced the Tiger Moth at the end of the war.

Restoration of these old warbirds is a painstaking job, and visitors are given a glimpse of the scope of the work involved when they look at the restoration of the Bristol Bolingbroke, a bomber that is being put together from eight cannibalized aircraft. This type of composite is necessary because Second World War aircraft were often left sitting in farmers' fields for forty years or so, remaindered after the war and bought by a farmer to use as a chicken coop or a source of wire and spare parts for farm equipment.

The most effective displays are those that lend a touch of personal history to the machinery, like the DC-3 Dakota, emblazoned with "Canuks Unlimited" for the squadrons who flew cargo drops in Burma during 1944-45. Along with the plane is a

*if you go*

DIRECTIONS: The Canadian Warplane Heritage Museum is at Hamilton Civic Airport, off Highway 6 at Mount Hope. The entrance to the museum is in Hangar 4. From the Queen Elizabeth Way take Highway 403 to Ancaster. Exit at Fiddlers Green Road and follow the signs.
SCHEDULE: Open daily year-round 10 a.m. to 4 p.m. The Tiger Squadron Canteen is open for snacks Saturday to Wednesday.
ADMISSION: Adults $4.25, students and seniors $3.25, children $2.25, children under 5 free.
INFORMATION: Call (416) 679-4183
MAP REFERENCE: 12

*classic collections*

## Canadian Warplane Heritage Museum

collection of Second World War snapshots showing the soldiers who were affiliated with it in Burma: bare-chested young men posing with a pet monkey, joking in front of a "Dew Drop Inn" signpost or exploring the overgrown ruins of a temple.

More than just aircraft can be seen here. Such period airfield equipment as fuel trucks and firehoses are all at hand, and some are still put to good use when the aircraft fly. Long tables at the perimeter of the building are used for folding parachutes. Visitors who come on Saturdays can often watch this being done.

A gift shop sells everything from pricey Longines aviator watches like the one worn by Charles Lindbergh to airplane models and magazines. One of the outbuildings has been refitted to look like an airmen's bar and now serves as a snack bar. The decor fits the theme, complete with its gallery of recognition, a wall of photographs showing people affiliated with the RCAF. The museum welcomes photo contributions to the gallery.

## *Kleinburg Doll Museum, Kleinburg*

The knack of a true collector is anticipating which items in today's junk will become tomorrow's treasure. Things that seem commonplace when they are first made become highly valued because they conjure up vivid memories and bring on powerful waves of nostalgia. Like the four Beatles dolls in Mary Gres's Kleinburg collection. They are just cheap plastic figures with bobbing heads, but there are many visitors who would love to acquire a set just like them — if they could. Mrs. Gres has had plenty of offers, but these souvenirs remain an important part of her collection of almost 200 dolls, some with pedigree credentials, others with junkshop backgrounds, but all very collectible.

Although the collection is rather compactly displayed in one room adjacent to Mrs. Gres's antique shop, it is remarkably comprehensive. It boasts dolls from Europe, Japan and North America by many important dollmakers as well as many interesting and unusual related items. The dolls are divided into categories such as babies, little girls, fashion ladies and character dolls. More than 100 of Mary's antique dolls, made of bisque, china, wax and other fragile materials, are displayed in glass cases. All the dolls are attired in period dress.

The oldest is an 1870 lady with an unusual head of molded china complete with what the dollmakers termed "sausage curls" of china hair. Also from that period is an English crèche baby made of wax, with glass eyes. Easy to sculpt and remarkably lifelike, wax was a popular medium for early dollmakers. It could be worked in various ways, either poured into a mold to form a solid shape or coated over a paper-mâché base. The 1880 pumpkin head is a wax fashion doll that takes its name from a seemingly oversize head resulting from the bouffant-style wax hair. Because wax melts so easily in a hot attic, very few of these dolls remain.

Perhaps the classic medium for doll-making is bisque, an unglazed porcelain that can be delicately hand-painted. Dolls are often fitted with wigs of human hair and elaborately costumed. The first doll Mrs. Gres acquired was a German bisque girl made by Simon and Halbig around

*classic collections*

## Kleinburg Doll Museum

the turn of the century. Like most bisques of its vintage, it is remarkably detailed, right down to the pierced ears. A bisque head called Flora Dora, by famed dollmaker Armand Marseille, is so detailed that it has eyebrows made of fur. Particularly precious are the French bisque dolls, prized for their exotic-looking faces, like the Limoges figures of the early 1900s with their prominent and vibrant features. Typical of the French style is a rare 1915 bisque by J. Verlinique with its large eyes, sculpted features and an expression that seems almost saucy. By comparison, many of the German dolls of that period are fuller faced and childlike.

It is in the facial expression that you can see the real art of doll-making, particularly in the character babies, like the 1910 German Lori baby, whose eyes seem uncannily real. They are known as intaglio eyes, made with the irises indented; this gives the effect of a lifelike, watching eye.

Also curious are the Japanese dolls made by Morimare Brothers in the early 1900s. While the baby doll looks vaguely Oriental, the little girl is totally Western, with her curly brown hair and round eyes. It was obviously designed for the export market.

Among the most popular dolls in the collection are the Eaton's Beauties, remembered as childhood favourites by many Canadian women. Mrs. Gres has six different models of the doll, a new edition of which was featured in each year's catalogue. Early ones were made of bisque, but in later years a composition of sawdust and glue was used; it didn't break as easily, but it tended to crack and peel when exposed to heat and moisture over the years.

Many of the valuable dolls in Mrs. Gres's collection were expensive bisque beauties even when they were new. They are much more precious now. An exception is a pair of German penny dolls so named because of their original price. Primitive wooden dolls with flexible joints, they were once commonplace, but now they too are considered precious.

In a Character Corner Mrs. Gres displays about seventy dolls (including the bobbing-head Beatles) that are relics of pop cultures past. There is a full-size Charlie McCarthy ventriloquist's puppet, a Howdy

Doody doll, two Kewpies, and an Emmett Kelly clown doll. A regal touch is provided by the Queen Elizabeth coronation souvenir doll made by Peggy Nisbet. From the sports world there are Barbara Ann Scott and Sonja Henie, both with figure skates.

Dolls were often used in commercial promotions, like the Campbell's Soup kids and the rubber Gerber baby seen in this collection. Another promotion piece popular in Toronto homes in the 1960s was a convict doll, once given away to anyone who bought an appliance from a company who claimed its prices were a steal. The freebie doll, it turns out, is the real steal, now worth about $50.

*if you go*

DIRECTIONS: The Kleinburg Doll Museum is in the village of Kleinburg on the main street, 10489 Islington Ave. From Toronto drive north either on Islington Ave. or on Highway 27 to Kleinburg, a distance of about 10 km (6 miles).
SCHEDULE: Open year-round, Tuesday to Sunday and holiday Mondays, noon to 5 p.m.
ADMISSION: Free.
INFORMATION: Call (416) 893-1358
MAP REFERENCE: 8

## *The Canadian Automotive Museum, Oshawa*

The North American love affair with the car continues despite rising gas prices and the arguments of conservationists. A visit to Ontario's automotive capital offers a retrospective look at this love affair, which says as much about the drivers as it does about their cars.

At the Canadian Automotive Museum in Oshawa all the paraphernalia of motoring is assembled alongside the machines, making it as much a display of social history as of technology. Anyone expecting a rusty old history of headlights is in for a pleasant surprise when they see the sixty-five autos, many of them vintage classics, surrounded by the artifacts of their eras. The museum owns over eighty cars but displays only sixty-five of them at any one time.

Many are simply esthetically pleasing. Take one look at the shiny blue 1911 Cadillac Model 30 Speedster and you are bound to fall in love. This car positively gleams, with its brass lamps and brass steering column, copper tubing in the engine and black leather seats.

The simplicity of many early models is very appealing. The 1902 Orient Buckboard didn't even have a steering wheel. Instead, a lever, looking much like a plane's throttle, was used to steer it. The 1903 Redpath Messenger was an early Canadian attempt to enter the automotive industry; it featured a single-cylinder engine and a top speed of 10 m.p.h.

Looking at these vintage autos certainly can make you nostalgic for a mythical golden era of motoring, whether it's embodied by the down-to-earth practicality of the Model-T or the glamour of the Cadillac. Nostalgia is not restricted to those able to remember their escapades in rumble seats, either. Even though there are cars dating back to the turn of the century — an 1898 Fisher Electric, for example — there are also plenty of newer models on display, including a 1981 Plymouth K Car, favourite of family drives, and a red 1966 Mustang, fit for burning rubber.

Rather than simply sticking them in a showroom setting, the museum displays the cars in a large social context. Old dance-band music fills the museum, and an assortment of antiques is displayed, including a wringer washer, a coal-burning cook stove and a vintage jukebox. Settings have been created for several of the cars, making them part of a tableau. An old-time garage front frames the 1911 Ford Roadster Model-T. A mock-up blacksmith shop (the earliest garage) is the backdrop for a dusty 1930 Marquette with a few strands of straw sticking out of the engine for authenticity.

For sheer whimsy, nothing beats the 1965 sky-blue convertible Amphicar, a West German effort designed to travel at speeds of up to 75 m.p.h. — or 10 m.p.h. in the water, thanks to a watertight chassis and two propellors in the rear. No mere foolish fantasy at work here, the Amphicar was given a successful test drive across the English Channel. James Bond would have loved it. Unfortunately, consumers didn't. The price was so high that motorists could have bought both a car and a boat for less money.

Along with the fantasy cars are the practical vehicles, including a 1926 Whippet Coupe converted to a mobile workshop, one of the earliest of its kind. Many cars have become more compact over time, whereas the tanker truck seems to have quadrupled in size, if the 1925 Ford Model-TT tanker truck is anything to judge by. The retired British American Oil Co. model on display seems to hold a liquid cargo just large enough to fill a modern-day tanker's gas tank.

The most interesting anecdotes in automotive history tend to be the personal ones, such as the story of Byron Carter, inventor of the four-seater 1911 Cartercar. More

*if you go*

DIRECTIONS: The Canadian Automotive Museum is at 99 Simcoe St. S. in Oshawa. From Highway 401 take the Simcoe St. exit and drive north 1.5 km (1 mile).
SCHEDULE: Open daily year-round. Weekends and holidays 10 a.m. to 6 p.m, weekdays 9 a.m. to 5 p.m.
ADMISSION: Adults $5, seniors and students $4.50, children 6 to 11 $3.50, 5 and under free.
INFORMATION: Call (416) 576-1222
MAP REFERENCE: 6

## The Canadian Automotive Museum

significant than his beautiful invention were the circumstances of his death; a heart attack induced by crank-starting a stalled Cadillac. The tragedy prompted his friend Charles Kettering of GM's research department to develop the electric starter.

After seeing the cars, take a side trip to tour the home of the man who made many of them. Colonel R. S. McLaughlin pioneered the Canadian auto industry in 1908, when the McLaughlin Company produced 154 McLaughlin F's. With his automotive fortune he built a magnificent mansion known as Parkwood. (See page 87.)

## Cullen Gardens and Miniature Village, Whitby

To really see smalltown Ontario, you have to go to Whitby. That's where visitors will see the smallest small town Ontario has ever known: the tiny, perfect, miniature village at Cullen Gardens. Here among the exotically trimmed shrubs, the rose gardens and the honeyed smell of alyssum, the familiar feel of smalltown Ontario life is evoked with remarkable accuracy, from the red-brick Victorian farmhouse to the take-out fried chicken outlet.

At first the prospect of a model Ontario village seems just a childish amusement, but each of the 150 models is a precise 1:12 scale copy of an existing farm, home, shop or church in Southern Ontario. As visitors wander past the thigh-high barns and the plastic cows, they involuntarily find themselves wondering where they've seen that gas station or the little stone church.

All are reproduced with a sense of humour and attention to detail. A tiny television screen flickers in the appliance store in the commercial section of town, while the bank advertises interest rates of 5.5 percent. The sandwich shop is called Mr. U-Boat, and Uncle Len's Lucky Fried Chicken is a tiny version of the familiar red-and-white buildings that peddle secret-recipe fried chicken; it needs only the smell of overheated fryer fat to seem real.

A crew of seven people worked for two years to make the village houses of marine plywood, which is scored to create the illusion of bricks and mortar. Like their full-size counterparts, miniature houses are built to withstand the weather. Constant maintenance is necessary to reshingle roofs (often with miniature cedar shingles).

Thousands of meters of 12-volt wires and water hoses are carefully buried underneath the village grounds to provide the power to light up streetlamps and send water through the tiny firemen's hoses as they douse a burning model house flickering with electric flame.

Animated figurines mend a main street roof, play on a see-saw in the schoolyard and swat flies on their front porches. Real plants complement the mini buildings. A bed of daffodils in full bloom looks like a fairy-tale

## Cullen Gardens and Miniature Village

forest surrounding the small farmstead buildings, but other living plants look quite realistic. Carefully groomed cedar seedlings resemble old maple trees when they line the miniature roadside, and thumb-size sweet alyssum look like window-high shrubs next to a model of a suburban bungalow.

Throughout this landscape winds a railway serving two trains, one freight and one passenger. In this era of declining passenger service, there is also a four-lane highway on which cars really move (unless it is under construction). Their destination is the adjacent miniature cottage country, modeled after Muskoka with a real ferry boat, moving motorboats on puddle-size lakes, summer homes, campsites and an amazing model of the old Windermere Inn.

The village changes with the seasons. Two sets of mini people are needed for this, one dressed in summer gear, the other clad for cold. On the fringes of the miniature town are suburbs where modern bungalows boast spacious lots and backyard pools. Just like the real ones, these pools all get winterized with little plastic covers.

For Christmas the tiny town is draped in miniature lights and features a Santa Claus parade with twenty-six floats, many animated copies of the ones in the old Eaton's parade in Toronto. Evening is a popular time to visit when the village and adjoining park are illuminated with about 100,000 lights. Mini streetlamps and tiny headlights on cars help light the way. Visitors walk

### if you go

**DIRECTIONS:** Cullen Gardens and Miniature Village is on Taunton Rd., north of Whitby. From Highway 401 exit at Highway 12 (Brock St.) and drive north to Taunton Rd., then turn west.

**SCHEDULE:** Open daily April to first week of January. April to mid-May 10 a.m. to 6 p.m., mid-May to mid-June 10 a.m. to 8 p.m., mid-June to mid-September 9 a.m. to 10 p.m., mid-September to mid-November 10 a.m. to 5 p.m., mid-November to early January 10 a.m. to 10 p.m.

**ADMISSION:** Adults $8, seniors and students $7, children $3.75, children under 4 free.

**INFORMATION:** Call (416) 668-6606 in Whitby or (416) 294-7965 in Toronto.

**MAP REFERENCE:** 6

152 *classic collections*

through 9 hectares (22 acres) of sculpted topiary shrubs and Christmas tableaux.

In spring there are the shows of tulips and other flowering bulbs. Come summer the roses are in bloom, followed by chrysanthemums in mid-September. During warm weather a miniature amusement park comes to life, with voices beckoning visitors to try their luck at games of chance and skill. A merry-go-round spins to the sound of carnival music as horses bob. Among the miniature midway rides is a model of the Canadian National Exhibition's famous Flyer, fully operational.

## *Aberfoyle Antique Market, Aberfoyle*

From kitsch to classic, the Aberfoyle Antique Market has it all. The longest-running (thirty-seven years as of 1992) antique market in Ontario, it unfailingly draws people on Sunday afternoon visits to this village of old stone buildings south of Guelph to browse and buy. There's a sweet smell of summer hay in the air as about 110 vendors peddle porcelain, pottery, pine and just about anything else that comes their way.

Within seconds of arriving you will find that prices here make the drive from Toronto worthwhile. Although the goods change from week to week, I've found everything from a $25 tea set of fine porcelain patterned with bluebirds to Art Deco dining-room suites. An unpriced taxi meter — still ticking — may not find a buyer easily, but there did seem to be a fair bit of interest in a 1916 Beaver sewing machine that operates on treadle power.

Caught studying a twenty-piece glass punchbowl set from some unspecified era, I was invited to put in an offer by a vendor eager to expatiate on the virtues of the accompanying sandwich plates. Just the thing for a Victorian-style garden party with crustless cucumber sandwiches.

Most vendors are content to let browsers have a good look, but they also are happy to offer quickie lessons in buying and collecting antiques. At one stall where Depression-era glass was featured, I was told that the cheaply manufactured glass pieces used as promotional giveaways by soap companies and movie houses during the Dirty Thirties are worth good money today. Identified by such patterns as the waffle or the iris, the glass pieces are now much in demand, and it is not unusual to pay $25 or $30 for such a glass pitcher.

Antique and flea markets are a good way of gauging technological change. The slide rule, an essential tool in every high-school math class just over a decade ago, is now to be found in piles of cheaper "nostalgia" items. Thanks to the pocket calculator, it's about as obsolete as the inkwell.

You don't need to be a serious collector to find something irresistible here. Kitsch lovers went into raptures of delight when they

*classic collections*

saw the salt-and-pepper shaker selection — red ceramic lobsters, a bear holding a salmon, two chipped chickens — all still functioning as seasoning sprinklers for under $5.

The diversity of the market also attracts people who need to buy things that just can't be found in ordinary stores. Need more 78s for the old Victrola? How about refill cards with scenic views for the stereoscope? Or a strange tap size to fit your turn-of-the-century plumbing? Chances are they'll be found at Aberfoyle.

### if you go

DIRECTIONS: The Aberfoyle Antique Market is in Aberfoyle. From Highway 401 exit at Brock Road 46 and drive north 3 km (2 miles) to Aberfoyle.

SCHEDULE: Open Sundays, May to October, 8 a.m. to 5 p.m.

ADMISSION: Adults $1.

INFORMATION: Call (519) 763-1077

MAP REFERENCE: 17

## Museum and Archives of Games, Waterloo

Few people outside Waterloo have ever heard of it, and it is so out-of-the-way that no one would ever happen upon the place by simply driving past. But the Museum and Archives of Games, tucked away in the University of Waterloo, is truly a hidden treasure, the only museum of its kind in Canada.

Before I had even walked in the door I could hear squeals of delight and anguish from visitors wrestling with brain teasers in a puzzle exhibit. The museum's proportions are modest: the gallery is no bigger than a school classroom. But its displays are entertaining enough to keep first-time visitors busy playing — and learning — for at least two hours.

Boasting a collection of approximately 5,000 artifacts, ranging in age from ancient Egyptian senet (a gambling game) to modern-day computer games, the museum displays its brain-teasing bounty in themed exhibits, usually three a year.

Past successes have included the History of Pinball, Pub Games, Inuit Games and the Great Puzzle Exhibit, which covered puzzle history from ancient Chinese tangrams to modern Rubik's Cubes. Playing With Television featured games based on TV shows. Displays are always given interesting didactic interpretation, so visitors to the puzzle exhibit, for example, learned that tangrams, a puzzle of shapes arranged into a variety of pictures, was a game enjoyed by both Napoleon and Edgar Allan Poe.

Many displays invite participation, whether it be disentangling oneself from knotted ropes, assembling wooden shapes or simply contemplating the answer to a word game. Although most displays are geared for adults and older children, there is usually at least a small selection of items for tots, like Sesame Street puzzles.

The museum's collection includes some extraordinarily valuable and finely crafted pieces, including a Victorian whist counter made of filigreed silver, tortoiseshell and ivory, as well as a finely carved Pacific Northwest Indian game counter shaped like a whale.

Coming exhibits are Gender Specific Games and An Electronic

Retrospective, featuring all those early computer games, such as Pac Man, that have so quickly become museum pieces.

### if you go

DIRECTIONS: The Museum and Archives of Games is in Kitchener-Waterloo at the University of Waterloo. With no signs to point the way the museum is difficult to find. It is on the ground floor of B. C. Matthews Hall. Enter the campus via Columbia St. and park in parking lot "N".

SCHEDULE: Open year-round but days and hours vary with each exhibit, so call ahead.

ADMISSION: Free. But be sure to bring four quarters or a loonie for the coin-operated parking gate, as change machines are nowhere in sight.

INFORMATION: Call (519) 888-4424

MAP REFERENCE: 16

# flora & fauna

## *African Lion Safari and Game Farm, Rockton*

I had my camera poised, ready to get a super close-up shot of a zebra, when it leaned over and licked the lens. Shooting big game is so easy at the African Lion Safari that photographers will soon find themselves abandoning their telephoto lenses so they can snap wide-angle shots of the animals that wander within licking distance of their cars.

The safari park, between Cambridge and Hamilton, is a private game farm where the roles are somewhat reversed. Motorists drive through six adjoining compounds covering 140 hectares (350 acres), while animals wander around the compounds inspecting the passing parade of tourists, who must remain in their cars. If a buffalo decides to park itself on the gravel road, then motorists must wait patiently for the beast to move.

When I visited on a sunny summer afternoon the traffic was piled up like rush hour on the 401, except that instead of slowing down because of fender-benders, excited motorists were watching lions lounging in the sun.

Passing through double metal gates, visitors enter the first compound to watch exotic birds like the East African crowned crane, the griffon vulture and the emu. Not all animals are always visible: a cheetah may choose to snooze out of sight, having seen enough tourists for one day.

Many animals, though, come surprisingly close to the road, like the tigers toying with a rubber tire swing or sleeping in the hot sun only an arm's length from the roadway. Metal grids in the road separate compounds, preventing emu from straying into the lion's territory and keeping baboons from mingling with black bears.

The Canadian vegetation makes an odd residence for the African animals. Here a pride of lions inhabits a landscape of linden, ash and crab apple trees instead of the grasslands of the African veldt. But the animals adapt well to their new Canadian home, and as autumn approaches lions begins to grow heavier coats and gain extra weight to stay warm through winter.

Although the big cats are majestic beasts, the real fun begins when visitors drive through the baboon compound. Here troops of curious primates come right up the the cars to catch a free ride on the side-view mirror and to inspect the car's occupants. Despite repeated warnings not to feed the animals, some visitors roll down windows to dole out peanuts, a dangerous business since the powerful baboons — an adult male can weigh 55 kg (120 pounds) — have been known to eat animals as large as young gazelles. The occasional piece of chrome car trim lying by the roadside is testimony to the animals' strength.

Visitors do get a chance to roll down their windows in the neighboring compound where zebras, giraffes and elands (large antelope) seem uncommonly curious about the visitors. Many will stroll from car to car, sticking their heads into windows, licking an outstretched palm or even trying to munch the upholstery. Motorists are repeatedly warned that their cars may sustain some damage, and anyone with a vinyl top or some loose trim would be well advised to take the air-conditioned safari bus instead of driving their own cars through the compounds.

It took us over an hour to drive the 10-km (6-mile) gravel road through the safari reserve, with stops to meet zebras and deer, and traffic jams building up where the tigers frisked alongside the road or buffalo and yak lumbered in front of the cars. With much of that time spent sitting in a closed car, anyone driving a

> *if you go*
>
> **DIRECTIONS:** The African Lion Safari and Game Farm is on Safari Rd., roughly 20 km (12 miles) northwest of Hamilton. From Highway 401 exit south on Highway 6, then west on Safari Rd. to the game park.
>
> **SCHEDULE:** Open daily from late April to late October. July and August 10 a.m. to 5:30 p.m., other months weekdays 10 a.m. to 4 p.m., weekends and holidays 10 a.m. to 5 p.m. The park grounds remain open for at least two hours after the final admission.
>
> **ADMISSION:** Adults $13, seniors and youths $11, children 3 to 12 $9. The safari bus charges $4.50 for adults, $4 for seniors and youths, $3.50 for children.
>
> **INFORMATION:** Call (519) 623-2620
>
> **MAP REFERENCE:** 12

## African Lion Safari and Game Farm

vehicle without air-conditioning should plan to make their trip on an overcast day, to avoid sweltering in the sun — or take the safari bus.

Spending that much time cooped up in the car, kids can get pretty restless, and the Safari Park organizers have very sensibly provided two playgrounds where young ones can burn off steam. Older children scramble across rope ladders and push around punching bags, while youngsters tumble in a bin full of plastic balls and bounce on springy toys. Be sure to bring bathing suits for the water playground with its slides, fountains and wading pools.

Included in the price of admission are a pontoon boat ride to see monkeys as well as four different animal shows in outdoor theatres. Parrots — several of which are hatched at the park — are seen performing tricks like roller skating for peanut rewards. More educational is the birds of prey demonstration, which explains the hunting habits of raptors. Rare Canadian horses are seen in the Animals and Man show, and the intelligence of the Asian elephants is demonstrated in the Elephant Roundup.

## Kortright Waterfowl Park, Guelph

While bird-watchers trudge through rain-drenched woods and soggy swamps to add more species to their checklists, less adventurous bird lovers can get a close-up view of the birds without even needing binoculars by visiting the Kortright Waterfowl Park near Guelph. The park contains North America's foremost collection of waterfowl, with ninety-two native and exotic species. In fact, the bird-watching is so good here that wildlife artists, including Robert Bateman, have been known to come to take photographs, and serious decoy carvers from Michigan have come for close-up observation of their models.

The 45-hectare (116-acre) park, owned by the Grand River Conservation Authority and operated by the Niska Wildlife Foundation, makes bird-spotting easy — and you'll see many species that local birders won't. The Egyptian goose, the Brazilian teal and black swans from Australia are just a few of the more exotic species.

Before visitors even see a goose they hear it. As they amble down to the bird compound they are greeted by frenzied honking, squawking and chirping. Dozens of curious geese look up from their foraging to see who is coming, then after a cursory hiss and flap they blithely waddle back to the water, ignoring the human visitors.

Visitors share the 2 km (1 1/4 miles) of gravel paths and boardwalks with roving geese and ducks. For the most part, the park looks like a wilderness, complete with croaking frogs and a network of gurgling streams crisscrossing the area. The more exotic fowl are kept in attractive pens that are artfully constructed to provide the most natural habitant. Waist-high fences make it easy to get a clear view of such land-bound birds as the green-beaked cereopsis geese and black swans whose flight feathers are clipped each year.

There are plenty of birds to be seen year-round, but come fall the park's 1,200 permanent residents are joined by flocks of migrating geese and as many as 5,000 migrating ducks. Wildfowl are attracted to the park largely because of its attractive location in the middle of a federal bird

## Kortright Waterfowl Park

sanctuary, surrounded by cornfields and fed with the waters of Hanlon Creek and numerous ponds. In spring there is the joy of watching the downy young parade behind their parents. By late May nesting is at its peak, with many young hatching and males still in their bright spring plumage.

Hatching is a serious business at this park, which raises roughly 1,000 ducklings, goslings and cygnets each year. Some of these birds will be used to replace park stock, others will be released in the wild, and some will be sold to zoos.

Not all ducks make good parents. Some of those species that might not be trusted to provide good mothering have their eggs removed and entrusted to the care of call ducks. The call ducks, a cross between domestic and wild, are good parents who will hatch the breeding species' eggs as if they were their own. In fact, they are thought not to know the difference.

If the Great Creator has a sense of humour, it certainly came out in the creation of ducks. Few sights are as comical as a flock of ducks waddling down a hiking path through these cedar woods. Watching quacking, flapping ducks coming in for a splash-landing on the pond is an entertainment that can keep visitors amused for hours. To this end, benches are thoughtfully positioned so that visitors can watch in comfort as exotic fowl swim alongside the more common species. A guidebook is essential for anyone who wants to identify the birds. The park provides a checklist, though it does not include descriptions of the birds, and there are few signs to let you know what you are seeing. To help you identify birds, the park office sells *A Coloured Key to the Wildfowl of the World*, by Peter Scott, for $21.

Many species of ducks that still have their flight feathers are kept in an enclosed duck pen, which in spring looks like a waterfowl condominium. Dozens of nesting boxes are fixed on poles rising out of the water. Some are equipped with a plank leading down to the water to create a habitat suitable for such ground breeders as blue-winged teal and pintails. Other boxes, placed higher on the same pole, simulate the cavity nests of bufflehead ducks, which prefer to lay their eggs in old woodpecker holes.

Waterfowl may be the park's specialty, but they aren't the only birds you'll find here. In addition to the freeloading pigeons, there are wild turkeys.

The park office has become a refuge for wounded birds of all species. Visitors may see anything from an injured hummingbird to a blue jay being trained to eat insects so it can fend for itself in the wild.

While watching the birds you might well find yourself being watched by one of the ten white-tailed deer that roam the park. Several are tame enough for you to pet.

Visitors are requested not to bring old bread to feed the birds, since it is difficult for them to digest.

### *if you go*

**DIRECTIONS:** The Kortright Waterfowl Park is south of Guelph at 305 Niska Rd. From Highway 401 drive north on Highway 6, then turn west on Niska Rd.

**SCHEDULE:** Open daily from May 1 to September 30, 10 a.m. to 5 p.m.

**ADMISSION:** Adults $2.15, seniors $1.90, students $1.60, children $1.10.

**INFORMATION:** Call (519) 824-6729

**MAP REFERENCE:** 17

# Jack Miner Sanctuary, Kingsville, and Point Pelee National Park, Leamington

As bird-watching becomes increasingly popular, more people are training their binoculars on Southern Ontario. Here they can visit a waterfowl sanctuary built by pioneering conservationist Jack Miner, and about 25 km (15 miles) to the east they can join naturalists spotting migrating birds at Point Pelee National Park.

The wild Canada goose is so closely tied to our national image that it seems difficult to imagine it ever vanishing, yet the bird came perilously close to extinction at the turn of the century, when overzealous hunters nearly sent it the way of the passenger pigeon. Today the honkers are back in full force, thanks largely to the efforts of Jack Miner.

Known fondly as Wild Goose Jack, Miner, a former hunter himself, gave up the sport when he noticed the numbers of Canada geese dwindling. The story of his personal efforts to save the birds are particularly relevant in these ecologically conscious times. Back in 1904 he was a pioneer in conservation when he tried to help migrating fowl by providing a resting pond. Four decoys were set out to attract the birds, but none showed up. He persisted, and slowly their numbers grew. Now about 30,000 geese are expected to stop at the Kingsville sanctuary on their southward journey from the Canadian Arctic to Chesapeake Bay and the Mississippi Valley.

Although the geese have come to be a common sight in city parks, many people still make the journey to Kingsville to see them en masse at the Jack Miner Sanctuary. On an autumn afternoon, hundreds of visitors turn up for a close-up view of the honkers. Sheltered viewing stands overlook a marshaling pond where birds are caught for banding. Youngsters are invited to feed some of the tamer waterfowl found dabbling in a pond in front of the Miner Museum, a two-story building filled with testimonials to Miner's extraordinary efforts. The display chronicles his pioneering work in bird banding when in 1909 he first secured an aluminum band to the leg of a mallard duck with a message that read "Write Box 48, Kingsville, Ont." so hunters could return the band and provide evidence of the bird's journey. The information gleaned from these banding projects led to the passage of legislation protecting the migratory birds. More than 2,000 geese are still banded here annually.

Geese and often swans congregate in an open field across the road from the museum, and every day at 3 and 4 p.m., weather permitting, someone drives an all-terrain vehicle slowly through the field to stir the thousands of wild birds into flight. Cameras click and tourists ooh and ahh as honkers take to the sky.

Jack Miner's conservation work has been so successful that the birds are prolific in many areas, especially along the migratory routes passing over Lake Erie. Bird-watchers make pilgrimages to the area, not only to see geese but to look for swans, hawks, assorted ducks and even

### *if you go*

**JACK MINER SANCTUARY**

**DIRECTIONS:** The Jack Miner Sanctuary is about 30 km (19 miles) southwest of Windsor. From Highway 401 take the Highway 77 exit south toward Leamington. At the arena, turn right onto Wilkinson Dr. and continue west through town, past Division Rd. to the sanctuary.

**SCHEDULE:** Museum open all year, Monday to Saturday 9 a.m. to 5 p.m. Bird migrations vary with the weather, so visitors should call ahead. Late October through November and late March are usually good times to see large numbers of geese.

**ADMISSION:** Free.

**INFORMATION:** Call (519) 733-4034

**MAP REFERENCE:** 22

**POINT PELEE NATIONAL PARK**

**DIRECTIONS:** Point Pelee National Park is roughly 50 km (30 miles) southeast of Windsor and approximately 35 km (22 miles) south of Highway 401, via Highway 77. At Leamington turn south on Road 33.

**SCHEDULE:** Open daily year-round, 6 a.m. to 10 p.m.

**ADMISSION:** April to Thanksgiving, $5 a car per day.

**INFORMATION:** Call (519) 322-2365 or (519) 322-2371.

**MAP REFERENCE:** 22

## Jack Miner Sanctuary and Point Pelee National Park

butterflies that fly through in early September.

Point Pelee National Park is the most famous of these sites. The southernmost point in mainland Canada, Point Pelee is a narrow spit of land that juts into Lake Erie, providing one of the narrowest crossings of the Great Lakes, thus shortening the treacherous flight over often stormy waters and making it a haven for many migratory birds.

The park's visitors' centre is well stocked with avian displays, books and even free checklists itemizing the 342 species that have been sighted in and around the park. Visitors are asked to chronicle their findings in the park's record books, and up-to-the-minute bird reports are posted on a board, keeping visitors alerted to all the latest bird activity, be it the nesting of an owl or the mating rituals of a mallard duck.

Point Pelee is a great place to see migrating monarch butterflies as well as hawks, owls and blue jays. At the beginning of October birders come here to see the red-breasted merganser (also known as the sawbill, for the serrated edge on its bill). As many as 30,000 have been seen in a single day. In spring the multicoloured warblers are the big draw.

## Kortright Centre for Conservation, Kleinburg

For urbanites at heart who might be put off by a canoe trip into blackfly-infested backwoods, the Kortright Centre for Conservation (not to be confused with Guelph's Kortright Waterfowl Park, named after the same conservationist) makes wildlife accessible and understandable. Although it is on the northwest fringe of Metro Toronto, it is a peaceful spot: 162 hectares (405 acres), including some scenic stretches of the Humber Valley. As you drive past the monster homes springing up like bad mushrooms all over this area, you get a sense of why this preserve is so important. This is a place where visitors can spot ducks, frogs and turtles. Deer are not unheard of at dawn and dusk, and even a wolf has been spotted.

You arrive to find a stunning and expansive visitors' centre, full of interesting displays that change throughout the season. You might stumble upon demonstrations of effective home insulation, bird feeder–building or acid-rain testing. A 150-seat theatre shows slide presentations relating to the current themes. There are often hands-on activities for youngsters, like making Inuit snow goggles or colouring paper leaves to paste on a tree.

It would be quite easy to enjoy the great outdoors from the comfort of the cafeteria, sipping coffee while watching the action at assorted bird feeders through the floor-to-ceiling windows. One section of the window is covered with mirror glass that has a shelf-style feeder on the other side. The birds are unaware of people, so visitors can watch them from only inches away.

More healthful, though, is a walk, or ski, along some of the 18 km (11 miles) of hiking trails. As seasons change, themed walks are planned. Two of my favourites are the wildflower walk in the spring, when naturalists show visitors dozens of otherwise difficult to spot little blooms, and the Myths and Magic hike that coincides with Halloween, when a naturalist imparts some unusual forest lore for casting spells.

Every hike has a point to make about wildlife. During the winter walks down Kortright's bird feeder trail, hikers learn about avian

## Kortright Centre for Conservation

nutrition and feeding habits, or to put it in urban terms, how to provide both the right menu and the proper ambience to lure birds to your own backyard bird feeder. A free pamphlet describes the attributes of the two dozen feeders along the trail.

Kortright is also the site of some interesting experiments in energy conservation, and visitors can hike up to an open field to examine assorted windmills and solar collecting devices. Once in a while a battery-operated car is brought out to demonstrate its efficacy. Visitors can walk through an energy-efficient demonstration cottage to learn how solar panels and a wind system provide electricity.

Also up in the field is an apiary, and during summer visitors can often see a beekeeper at work. From the safety of a screened room, visitors get a close-up look as the beekeeper opens the hives to collect honey. They learn about the delicate work of introducing a new queen to a hive, and can taste the honey produced here.

One of Kortright's biggest events is the annual Groundhog Day Winter Carnival, usually held the first weekend in February. Naturalists at the Kortright Centre have a knack for finding fascinating facts about any animal. In the groundhog's case there are some curious sexual habits to explore. Males and females sleep in separate burrows, and when the male awakes he goes looking for a female. His sense of smell is so strong that he can find her under more than a meter of snow.

That amount of snow is seldom seen at the Kortright Centre, but that doesn't spoil the winter fun. Visitors can usually join in a traditional Native game of throwing wooden snow snakes, play an Inuit tug-of-war game

---

*if you go*

**DIRECTIONS:** The Kortright Centre is near Kleinburg. From Highway 400 turn west at Major Mackenzie Dr., then south on Pine Valley Dr.

**SCHEDULE:** Open daily year-round, 10 a.m. to 4 p.m.

**ADMISSION:** Adults $4.25, children $2.25.

**INFORMATION:** Call Metropolitan Toronto and Region Conservation Authority at (416) 661-6600.

**MAP REFERENCE:** 8

and make crafts, like groundhog finger puppets.

The Kortright's biggest festival is the Four Winds Kite Festival, the first weekend in May, home to the Canadian National Stunt Kite Championships.

## Wye Marsh Wildlife Centre, Midland

There aren't many places where a bird-watcher can still see wild trumpeter swans in Ontario. In fact, the graceful giant was well on the way to joining the dodo until the Wye Marsh Wildlife Centre, near Midland, started a swan breeding program in 1988. Once plentiful in this province, these large birds have been known to weigh as much as 17 kg (38 pounds) and have a wingspan of 3 m (10 feet). There is a lot of meat on a bird that big, so when European firearms were introduced to North America, hunting the graceful swans became all too easy.

With the goal of reestablishing a wild migrating colony of swans in Ontario, a pair of trumpeter swans was brought from Michigan in 1988 to begin the breeding program. Their feathers were clipped and a spacious, swampy pen was built for them. The wire fence is not so much to keep the swans in (their clipped wings will do that) as it is to keep out such predators as snapping turtles and raccoons. Each spring the swans produce half a dozen eggs, which will hatch about a month later. The Ontario-born cygnets are free to migrate south in the fall and, it is hoped, will return the following spring, thus bringing wild swans back to the area after a two-century absence.

Visitors to Wye Marsh see the trumpeter swans while exploring the trails and boardwalk that wind through woodlands and wetlands. A 16-hectare (40-acre) corner of the 920-hectare (2,300-acre) marshlands is open to the public.

Wye Marsh naturalists are dedicated to convincing the public that a marsh is not just a watery wasteland waiting to be drained to create building sites, but a beautiful and useful part of the landscape that is teeming with life. Visitors are invited to pick up checklists, long-handled nets and bowls to use while exploring the marshlands. If you dip into the murky marsh water alongside the boardwalk you will scoop out what looks like a mess of slime. Closer inspection of the decaying weed and water will likely turn up such life as fingernail clams, spiral shell snails and mud minnows. It is not unusual to spot a green frog basking in the sunshine beside the boardwalk, a painted turtle resting on a decaying log or a snapping turtle sticking its pointed head out for air. Round brown mounds of vegetation look like piles of rotting matter; they are in fact home to the muskrats that can be seen swimming among the water grasses.

There is so much wildlife to watch here that renowned Canadian wildlife photographers John and Janet Foster have returned several times to film such remarkable footage as mink hunting a blue-winged teal.

But more than just a way to spot life forms, the nature walks become fascinating because the well-informed naturalists who lead them are a font of delightful information on ordinary things. Take, for instance, the humble duck weed. The tiny green flecks floating on the water look like mere pond scum, but they are the smallest flowering plant in North America, and are highly nutritious, containing more protein than soybeans. Duck weed, like cattails, also plays an important role in purifying water in the marsh reservoir by absorbing complex chemicals.

Perhaps the most appealing thing about a marsh is its primeval look. Some of the plants are truly primordial. Horsetails that grow like weird, stunted bamboo are sometimes referred to as dinosaur food because they have remained unchanged through the millennia.

Chances are that after you've spent a few hours roaming the boardwalks at Wye Marsh, you'll never look at a swamp the same way again. One of the myths happily debunked is that of the mosquito-infested marsh. In fact, the water is generally too deep for the pesky bugs to breed in. However, the pretty woodland trails lined with flowering shrubs, trillium, wild roses and jack-in-the-pulpits have no

### *if you go*

DIRECTIONS: The Wye Marsh Wildlife Centre is 5 km (3 miles) east of Midland. Take Highway 12 east from Midland to Wye Marsh (opposite the Martyrs' Shrine).
SCHEDULE: Open daily year-round, with cross-country skiing and snowshoeing in the winter. Mid-May to Labour Day 10 a.m. to 6 p.m., other times 10 a.m. to 4 p.m.
ADMISSION: Adults $4.50, seniors and students $3, children under 3 free.
INFORMATION: Call (705) 526-7809
MAP REFERENCE: 9

## Wye Marsh Wildlife Centre

shortage of the buzzing pests. To get some relief, and to learn more about the area, visit the indoor displays at the Wildlife Centre.

Throughout the year Wye Marsh holds many special activities. A few to watch for include the spring maple syrup harvest, guided canoe excursions, bird-watching trips, film series, art shows and guest speakers. The highlight is the annual Wildlife Festival of Conservation and Art, with everything from art shows to goofy contests like hip-wader races. In July and August visitors can register for hour-long canoe excursions guided by naturalists to look at aquatic plants and animals.

## Royal Botanical Gardens, Hamilton

The Royal Botanical Gardens proves that the steel city has its gentler side. These truly spectacular gardens cover 1,000 hectares (2,700 acres), straddling the boundary between Hamilton and Burlington and stretching up the Niagara Escarpment. Widely different plantings, themes, terrains and an exceptional greenhouse make this a year-round delight for nature lovers.

One of the best-known, and best-loved, sights is the springtime spectacle of flowering bulbs in the Rock Garden, where about 150,000 tulips, daffodils and other spring bulbs are artfully planted along the sheltered crags of a former gravel pit. The pit was redeveloped as a relief labor project during the Great Depression.

The Royal Botanical Gardens are so vast that you'll need a car to get from one specialty garden to the next. About 2 km (1 mile) from the Rock Garden is the arboretum, where the sweet scent of magnolia blossoms hangs in the May air. Here nature is organized into orderly, thematic plantings: hedge gardens, rhododendron gardens and collections of flowering trees. Best of all is the lilac dell, which is at its blooming best in mid- to late May when 700 kinds of lilacs flower. Gathered from gardens from Manitoba to Moscow, the lilacs bear florets varying from lacy white to rich purple, with variations of cream, pink and mauve in between. Music rings through the dell on Lilac Sunday (usually late in May), when an orchestra performs outdoors.

During summer months the 0.8-hectare (2-acre) Rose Garden comes into full bloom. In autumn nature lovers can walk some 50 km (30 miles) of trails through the Royal Botanical Gardens, including Cootes Paradise and Rock Chapel wildlife sanctuaries. Guided walks along these trails, as well as tips on bird-watching, wildlife identification and a host of other subjects, are offered through the arboretum's Nature Centre.

During winter visitors can escape to sunnier climes by visiting the Royal Botanical Gardens' Mediterranean Garden. Creating a miniature version of a terraced Mediterranean garden under glass on the outskirts of Hamilton is not quite as outrageous a project as it first seems. Since

## Royal Botanical Gardens

Hamilton is on the same latitude as the south of France, the year-round light conditions are identical. In early February, when snow squalls are stalling traffic on the nearby Queen Elizabeth Way, in the heated greenhouse many Mediterranean plants begin to bloom and set fruit.

Greenhouse visitors first walk through a Floral Hall, where the cool air is thick with the fragrance of hyacinths. A pretty tangle of blooms overflows from the beds; pink primula, tiny yellow iris and purple fuchsia among them. Pure white flowers adorn the camellia shrubs.

Stepping into the main greenhouse is like setting foot on a magnificent patio, with terra cotta tiles, urns and trellises, an elegant pool for oversize goldfish, and pots filled with shrubs and trees.

An impressive jasmine vine's white flowers perfume the air, and it's not the only fragrance stirring your nostrils. A massive bush of rosemary, covered with pale blue flowers, lemon thyme and sage are just a few of the herbs that add to the scent. It is startling to see how large many of these culinary plants can grow in natural conditions. A specimen of giant fennel, a plant usually seen sold with celery-size stalks, is well over 2 m (6 1/2 feet) tall. Many plants bear fruit: oversize Ponderosa lemons, pomegranates and bitter little calamondin oranges among them.

Gardeners may be particularly interested to see the wild ancestors of the hybrid plants found in Canadian gardens. Here they can see many species bulbs, including wild daffodils. Because several areas of the globe have what botanists call a Mediterranean climate, there are plants from all over the world, like freesia and geraniums from South Africa, eucalyptus from Australia and miniature wild iris from Turkey.

There are three full-time gardeners on duty during the week, as well as volunteers on the weekends, who are glad to answer questions. But you don't have to be a gardening buff or botanist to enjoy this sensuous greenhouse. Just spending a few minutes perched on a bench inhaling in the heady scent of jasmine is enough of a winter pick-me-up to make the visit worthwhile.

Whether visiting the gardens indoors or out, it is wise to stop first at the Royal Botanical Gardens Centre (also the site of the Mediterranean Garden) at 680 Plains Rd. The centre has pamphlets and maps describing the gardens' offerings. Since the assorted gardens are spread out over such a large area, it is important to get a clear idea of everything that is available. During warm weather a pretty place for lunch or a snack is the tea house overlooking the Rock Garden where the spring bulbs are planted.

### *if you go*

DIRECTIONS: The Royal Botanical Gardens Centre is at 680 Plains Rd. in Hamilton. From the Queen Elizabeth Way take Highway 403 west, then Highway 6 north. Turn right at the first light, then exit left onto Plains Rd. Follow the signs.

SCHEDULE: Open daily year-round. Outdoors, 9:30 a.m. to 7:30 p.m. Mediterranean Garden, 9 a.m. to 5 p.m.

ADMISSION: Outdoors: from mid-April to late-September, adults $4, children and seniors $3. Mediterranean Garden: from October to April, $2. Parking at Rock Garden $2.50 a car.

INFORMATION: Call (416) 527-1158

MAP REFERENCE: 12

## Arboretum Nature Centre, Guelph

While an arboretum is generally a planting of trees organized for scientific purposes, the University of Guelph's arboretum staff have added playfulness to that purpose by providing informative, year-round entertainments that transform this 165-hectare (410-acre) collection of trees, shrubs and vines into a great spot for a family outing.

This is a busy place, with a host of inventive programs organized by staff at the Arboretum Nature Centre. Visitors can join in a wide range of activities from watching warblers to weasels, honey bees to butterflies. Winter or summer, there is something interesting happening here, particularly on Sunday afternoons, when visitors can take guided walks and talks that feature a different theme each week. In winter they can explore trails on snowshoes borrowed from the Nature Centre (just bring ID).

If you prefer to wander on your own, go ahead and explore the 8 km (5 miles) of trails. These nature trails — one, Victoria Woods, has wheelchair access — may be explored year-round. A boardwalk winds through a marsh known as a good bird-watching spot. Maps are available in the Nature Centre.

The knowledgeable staff are great at helping to identify plants and animals to be found along the trails. Visitors are sure to see animals. At the very least chickadees at the bird feeders or, if you're lucky, a white-tailed doe and her fawn bounding through the collection of dwarf conifers.

Tree and shrub collections are organized into twenty-three family groupings such as oaks, rhododendrons, lilacs and maples. Particularly surprising to nonbotanists are the various plants that turn up in the same family group. It is a lesson in botany to sniff a fragrant rose, then learn that fruit trees also belong to the same rosaceous family. An apple is in fact a sort of rosehip. and the apple blossom is a type of rose.

Landscaping styles are varied to suit each collection. Dwarf conifers are arranged in an area of neatly manicured lawns, while native trees are in a more natural setting where the grass remains uncut. A split-rail fence surrounds what looks like an area gone wild but is in fact one of the collections, known as the Old Field, where nature appears au naturel. Asters, goldenrod, sunflowers and a myriad of other wildflowers thrive in this collection that has no gardener's intervention.

Wildlife lovers will appreciate the Gosling Wildlife Garden, specially designed to attract fauna. The appetites of assorted animals from butterflies to deer have been taken into account in selecting the species that produce acceptable fruits and foraging.

Children always enjoy a visit to the indoor Nature Centre with its displays geared to youngsters and its hive of live honey bees visible through a Plexiglas window, rats and a friendly rabbit.

> *if you go*
>
> **DIRECTIONS:** The Arboretum Nature Centre is on the campus of the University of Guelph, in Guelph. From Highway 401 take Brock Rd. north to the campus at Stone Rd. On campus follow South Ring Rd. to East Ring Rd.
>
> **SCHEDULE:** Open year-round, weekends 12:30 to 4:30 p.m. The best time to visit is Sunday afternoons to catch one of the programs.
>
> **ADMISSION:** Free.
>
> **INFORMATION:** Call (519) 824-4120, extension 3932.
>
> **MAP REFERENCE:** 17

## Mountsberg Wildlife Centre, Milton

One of Ontario's largest bird-banding stations, the Mountsberg Wildlife Centre makes it easy for families to get close to nature and to witness a massive bird-banding project in the spring and autumn. Banding 5,000 to 10,000 birds annually, this station has enabled scientists to trace the movements of many difficult-to-follow species. Anyone interested in the procedure should call to find out when the public bird-banding programs will be held each spring and fall. That's when you can observe naturalists retrieving birds caught in the fine mist nets and fitting them with metal leg bands.

Talking to naturalists, visitors gain some insights into the patterns of bird travel. One house finch banded at Mountsberg had flown all the way to Alaska within a month. Blue-winged teals banded here have been found in Cuba, Trinidad, Haiti and other southern climes.

Among the most impressive of Mountsberg's efforts is its banding of bobolinks, the pretty songbird known for its ebullient tune. These birds are not easy to catch, but Mountsberg naturalists have had great success luring them to fields planted with alternating rows of millet and sunflowers. Millet is among their favourite foods, but the plants are too flimsy to support the birds, so the sunflowers give them a place to perch while they eat. A wild birdseed garden near the Interpretive Centre gives visitors a few ideas for growing avian goodies.

Watching wild waterfowl is especially easy here, thanks to a large reservoir that makes a great splash-down spot for migrating birds. Wood ducks are particularly numerous here because of a nesting box program.

Mountsberg is also known for its efforts in rehabilitating wounded raptors. Visitors who follow a wildlife walkway will find an assortment of caged birds that typically includes turkey vultures, eagles, falcons, hawks and owls. Impressive herds of elk and buffalo can be seen grazing and lazing in their pens.

Taking a walk on the wild side here means ambling along a marsh-bound boardwalk to watch frogs laying eggs or turtles basking in the sun, following a moss-covered split-rail fence to look for clusters of violets or wandering through woods to find carpets of trillium and mayapple.

Throughout the year there are special activities designed to bring visitors into contact with wildlife, from frog watching to owl prowls. Cross-country ski trails wind through woodlands where chickadees flit through the evergreens. In March there's the sweet joy of riding to the sugar bush on a horse-drawn wagon and tasting the syrup. During summer there are 22 km (14 miles) of hiking trails to explore, and in the fall visitors can focus their binoculars on the migrating birds.

Spring is a great time for youngsters and bird lovers to visit. Then an old barn is busy with new life. Newborn lambs and goats will come to nibble on a trouser leg, and newly hatched chicks and Silkie hens peck about.

The modern Interpretive Centre boasts excellent displays explaining the area's wildlife. Here visitors can pick up free brochures and maps to help them find their way around the 440-hectare (1,100-acre) conservation area. A wildlife report board is posted at the centre for anyone to list their sightings. On a typical spring afternoon these might include an assortment of salamanders, snakes, ducks and hawks. Naturalists often lead theme walks or demonstrations, looking for wildflowers, amphibians or insects, hooting at owls or catching bats.

### *if you go*

DIRECTIONS: The Mountsberg Wildlife Centre is west of Milton. From Highway 401 exit south on the Guelph Line, then turn west on Campbellville Rd., to Milborough Town Line and look for the signs.

SCHEDULE: Open daily year-round, 10 a.m. to 4:30 p.m., with public programs on weekends.

ADMISSION: Adults $2.50, students $2, seniors and children $1.50, preschoolers free.

INFORMATION: Call (416) 336-1158 on weekdays, (416) 854-2276 on weekends.

MAP REFERENCE: 11

## Dorcas Bay Nature Reserve, Tobermory

The northern stretch of the Bruce Peninsula is blessed with a unique abundance of wildflowers, most notably orchids. In fact, orchids are said to occur here in greater abundance and with more diversity than almost anywhere else on the continent.

While it is perfectly easy to spot brilliantly coloured flowers, like the yellow lady's slipper, at the side of Highway 6, keen nature lovers will be rewarded by a visit to Dorcas Bay, one of the best-kept secrets on the Bruce. Unless a friend tells you about this wildlife preserve, it's not likely you would ever find this remarkable spot. Little in the way of brochures or signs advertises its existence. This is probably for the best, since the survival of many of these delicate blooms relies on their being undisturbed.

In 1962 the Federation of Ontario Naturalists acquired this 132-hectare (330-acre) property, one of the last stretches of natural Lake Huron shoreline, in order to protect it from development. During the summer a warden alternates between here and Petrel Point at Red Bay to the south. A sign simply announces, "Walkers welcome. Please leave plants untouched for others to see."

To really enjoy Dorcas Bay, go equipped with a guidebook — *Newcomb's Wildflower Guide* is recommended because flowers are grouped according to structure, rather than colour, for greater accuracy. Flower enthusiasts seem to be generous folk, sharing their finds and pointing out locations of seldom-seen blooms, which is a good thing, since many of the unusual species are not readily obvious.

The rare sundew, which at first glance looks like nothing more than a tiny clump of reddish leaves, would be easy to step on while one is searching for showier blooms, if it weren't for a little expert spotting. Anyone lucky enough to find it, though, has stumbled upon an unusual insectivorous plant that uses its sticky leaves to snare its buggy prey.

Carnivorous plants are typically thought to be a rare tropical phenomenon, but they turn up with surprising frequency in this Ontario habitat. Another fly-eater commonly found in and around Dorcas Bay is the pitcher plant, whose tube-shaped leaves hold pools of rainwater. Insects walk into the pitcher leaves and become trapped by its hairs. Even the tiny purple butterwort can trap flies with its sticky leaves.

For colour, nothing beats the show of Indian paintbrush, whose crimson tips stand out in a grassy field. In the woods, visitors might find a carpet of white bunchberry or purple-fringed polygala. Trails lined with wild strawberries, roses and blueberries look as though they provide ample meals for the wildlife that abounds here.

In spring and early summer that wildlife includes multitudes of blackflies and mosquitoes. Hats, long sleeves and insect repellant are essential. Despite the bug bites, Dorcas Bay offers many pleasures. Spruce and juniper scent the trails, and a steady breeze blows in off Lake Huron, where white sand beaches dotted with driftwood beg to be explored.

Dorcas Bay is a big favourite with photographers, and at every turn you see them dressed like safari game hunters with their multipocketed vests, tripods, light meters and long-lensed cameras that dwarf their delicate subjects. Photographers should be warned that eagerness to capture the perfect shot of the perfect bloom can be fatal to the plants. Dying vegetation should never be pushed aside for a better view of the bloom — it protects and nourishes many species.

According to experienced photographers, the flowers are generally at their best during early June, with pink lady's slipper rounding off the season in early July.

> *if you go*
>
> DIRECTIONS: Dorcas Bay is about 11 km (7 miles) south of Tobermory. From Highway 6 look for the sign pointing to Singing Sands Beach and follow the road to the end.
> SCHEDULE: Accessible year-round.
> ADMISSION: Free
> INFORMATION: Call the Federation of Ontario Naturalists, in Toronto, at (416) 444-8419.
> ACCOMMODATION: The most convenient town to stay in is Tobermory. It has a tent and trailer park as well as several motels. A personal favourite is the Grandview Motel, overlooking the harbour. (For details see Flowerpot Island, page 132.)
> MAP REFERENCE: 20

*flora & fauna*

## *favourite festivals*

## *Fergus Highland Games, Fergus*

Skirling bagpipes and swirling kilts make the town of Fergus seem very Scottish indeed. Every year the town celebrates its Celtic heritage with the World Class Championship Supreme Highland Games, which lure top competitors for a day of hammer-throwing, caber-tossing and stone-flinging. Massed bands and scores of kilted dancers make this as big a Scottish extravaganza you are ever likely to see on this side of the Atlantic.

In fact, Fergus's Highland Games have become such a success that they have grown beyond the athletic field and taken over the entire town for a whole weekend of Scottish celebrations, in the second weekend of every August.

A welcome tea awaits visitors arriving on Friday at the Fergus Legion Hall, where a hostess answers questions about the weekend schedule and local attractions. That evening Victoria Park is the site of a musical tattoo, with highland pipe bands, brass bands, marching bands, singers and dancers. Professional pipers enter the competition at St. Andrew's Presbyterian Church, blowing marches, reels and strathspeys (fast dances) for the gold medal. The 1862 stone church is noted for its good acoustics.

Of course the Highland Games remain the centrepiece of the celebrations, with an all-day program that starts Saturday at 8 a.m. in Victoria Park. The schedule remains much the same from year to year. Highland dancing, solo drumming and piping competitions continue throughout the day, but the really stirring music, the stuff that makes even non-Scots want to rush out and buy a kilt, is the spectacle of the massed bands led by drum majors decked out in bearskin caps and swirling capes. Opening ceremonies usually begin around 12:30 p.m., followed by the massed highland fling, with hundreds of dancers all performing simultaneously, then the massed bands. There is a second massed band finale at the closing ceremonies about 5 p.m.

You should come early to get a grandstand seat for a good view of the proceedings, and bring a hat because the stands are in full sun.

Many experienced games-goers bring their own lawn chairs for a seat on the shady hillside overlooking the stages where dancers compete.

The sporting highlight is the afternoon of heavy events. The term "heavy" describes not only the competition but the competitors: a dozen brawny men who each weigh over 250 pounds and stand more than 6 foot 2. Putting their muscles to the test, they heft assorted weights, including a 10-kg (22-pound) hammer (thrown for distance) and a 25-kg (56-pound) weight (tossed straight up). The biggest challenge is presented by the cumbersome cabers, like telephone poles, weighing 55 and 60 kg (120 and 135 pounds). Just picking up the pole from the ground with cupped hands is challenge enough, let alone hurling it end over end across a field.

A grueling contest that originated at Fergus is the Highland Games Walk, in which contestants carry 90-kg (200-pound) iron railroad rails, one in each hand, for the farthest distance possible, a feat that requires balance as well as strength.

Take a break from the sweltering stands to stroll through the market area where dozen of stalls sell reams of Scottish trappings from tartans to colourful clan histories and Scottish woolens. The selection of Scottish gear is both amazing and amusing. Where else could shoppers browse through an entire rack of bagpipe mouthpieces, tartan ties or a plenitude of literature on such obscure subjects as the history of the haggis?

If you suspect you might have Scottish connections, you can trace your roots with help from history buffs in the Avenue of the Clans. Clan representatives are on hand to answer questions about their tartans and septs (branches). Hungry visitors can snack on Scottish goodies such as bridies (meat pies) and Eccles cakes (currant-filled pastries), all washed down with Irn Bru (Scottish soda pop). In every corner of the park the nonstop drone of the bagpipes can be heard.

When the skirl of the bagpipes has left a near permanent ringing in your ears it is time to look at some of Fergus's other Scottish charms. Situated on the Grand River, this handsome town with its stone

## Fergus Highland Games

architecture comes by its Scottish celebrations with honest credentials. It was founded in the mid-nineteenth century by two wealthy Scots, Adam Fergusson and James Webster, who sought out other Scots of upstanding character to settle the area. Stonemasons soon erected gray limestone buildings that echo the architecture of their native land.

Some of that architecture can be seen on a short walk around town. Many of the houses have fascinating stories attached. Take the Groves' house, for instance. It was home to the first surgeon in North America to successfully perform an appendectomy, back in the 1880s. Success was certainly in part a result of Dr. Grove's innovative practice of sterilizing all equipment.

In a little cottage, settler Hugh Black lived with his thirteen children. An accountant by trade, Black arrived in the area with seven wagons full of furniture, and when the local folk saw the stuff they decided he had to be the man to open the tavern — no one else had enough chairs. So, obligingly, he did.

Not to be missed is Fergus's market, open Saturday and Sunday from 8 a.m. to 5 p.m. and located in an old stone warehouse on the banks of the Grand. In addition to farmers' produce, visitors will find crafts, antiques and what else but a Scottish shop that sells goodies like ginger marmalade.

Anyone who succumbs to the lures of the tartan and buys a kilt can always wear it to Sunday morning's kirkin' o' the tartan service at St. Andrew's, where the minister performs a service dating back to the time when the English outlawed the tartan. Loyal Scots would bring a hidden scrap to church and the

*if you go*

DIRECTIONS: Fergus is north of Guelph via Highway 6. Follow the signs to Victoria Park.
SCHEDULE: The Highland Games are held on the second weekend in August.
ADMISSION: Tickets are $8 to $12 for adults, $3 for children.
INFORMATION: For details on the games and accommodations call the Fergus Chamber of Commerce at (519) 843-5140.
MAP REFERENCE: 17

minister would bless the tartan in Gaelic so no Englishmen could understand. A sampling of Scottish entertainments from singing to sheep dog trials rounds out the Sunday afternoon.

# Black Creek Pioneer Village Pioneer Festival, North York

In an age when many fall festivals now boast demolition derbies, rock concerts and thrills-'n'-spills midway rides, the old-fashioned fun of a rural harvest celebration often seems tame. But at Black Creek Pioneer Village's annual Pioneer Festival you can still get a slice of homebaked pie, enter your kids in the spelling bee and experience life at a simpler and slower pace.

Going strong since 1956, the annual Pioneer Festival is one of the biggest and most popular events at Black Creek Pioneer Village, on the northwestern edge of Metro Toronto. With its dirt roads, wooden plank sidewalks and more than forty nineteenth-century homes, farm buildings and businesses, Black Creek Pioneer Village makes the perfect setting for the old-fashioned Pioneer Festival, which is a major fundraiser for the Mennonite Central Committee. The committee uses the monies for Third World development and relief.

Experienced festival-goers come early and come hungry, because this is an event renowned for its heaping helpings of Mennonite and Pennsylvania German foods, including pies, preserves, butter tarts, apple fritters, barbecued chicken, sauerkraut, sausages, cheeses and breads. Not only is it a finger-licking feast but it's a great shopping opportunity for city folk who can enjoy a country-style market come to the city. Farmers set up an outdoor market in the village, selling locally grown produce.

At noon on Festival Day the old drive shed becomes the stage for an auction of handmade Mennonite quilts in traditional patterns like the lone star. They are just a few of the handmade crafts on sale that day.

During the Pioneer Festival, and throughout the year, visitors can tour through the village's old shops to see almost-forgotten crafts like tinsmithing and broom-making. In the old homes they get a sense of the hardships and the triumphs the early settlers faced. A special favourite is Daniel Stong's first house, a rude 1816 log cabin where guides still occasionally cook over the open hearth, using long-handled utensils and huge kettles suspended over the flames. Nearby are the smokehouse, so essential to the Stongs' preparation of a winter supply of meat, and the root cellar for keeping produce.

Oxen, like the pair usually seen in the barnyard, were used to clear tree stumps, then plow fields, although the present-day pair seem to enjoy no task more strenuous than posing for tourists.

Children are alternately amused and horrified to get a taste of nineteenth-century school life at the 1861 one-room Dickson's Hill School, where scholars wrote on slates with slate pencils to spare the expense of paper. Spelling contests were a popular Friday afternoon endeavor, and during the festival youngsters can compete in an old-fashioned spelling bee.

The festival is also the time to see soldiers in period costume on the village green. In the highly regimented fashion of nineteenth-century combat they load and fire muskets.

The Pioneer Festival is just one of dozens of special events staged at Black Creek throughout the year. Also popular are the Christmas celebrations, which highlight an impressive nineteenth-century toy collection as well as a visit with Santa, who invites youngsters to write a letter or help in his workshop.

### *if you go*

**DIRECTIONS:** Black Creek Pioneer Village is at Jane St. and Steeles Ave. in northwest Metro Toronto. From Highway 400 exit at Steeles and drive east.

**SCHEDULE:** The Pioneer Festival is usually held from 10 a.m. to 4 p.m. on the second or third Saturday in September. The village's historic buildings are open from mid-March to December. Only the grounds and Visitors' Centre are open winter weekends for sleigh rides. Hours vary, so call ahead for details.

**ADMISSION:** Adults $6.50, seniors $4, students and children 5 to 15 $3.

**INFORMATION:** Call (416) 736-1733

**MAP REFERENCE:** 7

# Sharon Temple Feast Days and Illumination, Newmarket

One of this province's most joyful places, the Sharon Temple provides a pretty setting for some unique festivities dating back to the time of the area's settlers. Sitting like a three-tiered wedding cake, the temple is not only a lovely historic site but one that is custom-built for musical celebration.

The 1831 house of worship was built by a religious sect, the Children of Peace, who had a particular interest in music. Led by David Willson, the Children of Peace were an offshoot of the Quakers who came as Loyalists to Upper Canada. Willson rebelled against the Quaker restriction against music and came to Canada from New York in 1801 to take advantage of free land grants.

Despite losing all their possessions in a shipwreck, David Willson and his wife headed, undaunted, up Yonge St. and into the virgin forest. In the woods of Upper Canada he soon found friends to share his liberal views and love of music, so he started the Children of Peace, who celebrated their love of God in musical worship. Successful settlers, Willson and his followers thrived and by 1825 had begun to erect their 25-m (82-foot) high temple.

Artfully constructed, the temple is not only a visual delight but also acoustically excellent, a fact that led to the founding of the present-day Music at Sharon festival in July. (The successful festival eventually outgrew the temple and is now held at Sharon Hope United Church.) The temple's graceful architecture was widely celebrated in its time.

In Willson's day the temple was used only fifteen times a year for feasts, once each month and at Christmas, one extra evening in September and an early June feast that coincided with Willson's birthday. Museum staff have reintroduced some of those feasts, and they have become extremely popular. The first Sunday in June is the traditional birthday celebration for Willson, with a Silver Band (similar to what would have been popular at the period) performing on the grounds.

Truly beautiful is the Illumination, on the first Friday of September, when a candle is lit at dusk in every window of the building to symbolize the light of the gospel. Inside there are readings and a historical talk, and choirs perform as they would have in Willson's day. This special evening is extremely popular. Tickets are limited and must be booked in advance.

Not a traditional festival for the Children, but incredibly popular with modern-day visitors, is the three-day Thanksgiving weekend Harvest Festival, a family-oriented celebration featuring such pioneer skills as dying, spinning and cider-making on an old wooden press. Mulled cider is served to visitors, a perfect accompaniment to all the home baking.

You don't need to wait until festival time to tour the magnificent temple. From May to October you can take a guided tour. Built in graduated tiers, the temple's three square stories represent the Holy Trinity. Twelve pillars inside symbolize the Apostles, while doors on all four sides admit people from every direction on an equal footing.

Tour guides enjoy an opportunity to wind up the rare 1820 barrel organ for visitors. This offbeat instrument operates on a principle similar to that of a player piano. Someone simply churns out tunes by cranking a handle. Also restored is a more conventional keyboard organ.

Visitors can stroll the grounds to see some of the other buildings that once belonged to the sect, among them David Willson's one-room study, a charming building whose clean design complements the temple. Although Willson's house no longer stands, his privy has been reerected behind the Doan House, also on the temple grounds. A walk through the herb garden reveals an unusual circular building that looks more like a miniature lighthouse than an outhouse.

Doan House is the simple but elegant clapboard home of Ebenezer

*if you go*

DIRECTIONS: The Sharon Temple is in the village of Sharon, on Leslie St. Sharon is 4 km (2 1/2 miles) north of Newmarket. From Highway 11 turn east at Road 13 to Sharon.

SCHEDULE: Open from May to October, Saturday to Thursday 11 a.m. to 5 p.m.; daily during July and August.

ADMISSION: Adults $3.25, seniors and teens $2.25, children $1.

INFORMATION: Call (416) 478-2389

MAP REFERENCE: 8

## Sharon Temple Feast Days and Illumination

Doan, the master builder of Sharon Temple. Inside the house, costumed guides are sometimes seen baking tea biscuits while they chat with visitors about Doan's architectural innovations, like bedroom closets.

An exhibition hall tells the story of these early settlers. Displays of tools show that the same craftsmanship used in building the temple was brought to everyday items like a pitchfork fashioned from a single pole. Though David Willson was a pacifist, many of his followers joined William Lyon Mackenzie in his failed 1837 rebellion to protest government corruption. Facing charges of treason, the rebels whiled away their time in jail by carving little wooden boxes, several of which are on display.

## Wikwemikong Pow Wow, Manitoulin Island

The annual Wikwemikong Pow Wow on Manitoulin Island is probably one of the finest festivals in this province, but very few non-Native people have ever heard of it, let alone attended it. Although it is a famous pow wow, attracting Native people from across North America, it receives very little publicity.

Maybe that's what makes it so good. This is not a commercial tourist attraction, but an honest celebration of traditional Native culture that just happens to welcome non-Native visitors who are lucky enough to find out about it.

Every August Civic Holiday weekend the only unceded reserve in North America — Manitoulin Island Indian Reserve, on the beautiful eastern peninsula of the island — hosts this pow wow, which attracts scores of Native dancers and drummers to the village of Wikwemikong. A dusty baseball diamond is transformed with spruce boughs and sawdust into a stage for dancers, where drummers beat out hypnotic rhythms under a cedar canopy on the third base line. Throughout the weekend the audience comes and goes from the bleachers while the dancing, drumming and singing continue.

Keen pow wow-goers arrive by Friday night to mingle with the performers as they warm up for a weekend of dancing. By Saturday morning the grounds surrounding the baseball diamond start to fill up. Vendors set up stalls selling shell earrings, porcupine quill boxes, sweetgrass braids, moccasins, and mittens decorated with tufts of moose hair. All the crafts are genuine Native work.

By Saturday noon everyone is ready for the grand entry parade led by an elder bearing the Native flag and staff. Following him, war veterans proudly march in with chests full of medals, then men, women and children all costumed for a weekend of traditional dancing. As teams of drummers pound out rhythms and chant, the line of dancers snakes around the stage. The emcee urges everyone to dance, and even tots in diapers can't resist the urge to bob with the beat.

As well as being social, the dancing is competitive. Throughout the

## Wikwemikong Pow Wow

weekend judges watch competing dancers with an eye to their movements, enthusiasm and costumes. Dancers compete in several categories divided by age and gender, traditional and fancy dress. The traditional dancers wear costumes drawn from Native legend and nature, with eagles' feathers worn like medals on a headdress or bustle, perhaps bearing a turtle-shell rattle or a bear-claw necklace.

Fancy dress, which is popular with young, athletic dancers, is characterized by flamboyant colours and a plethora of feathers that seems to fit the Hollywood stereotype of what an Indian costume should be. By contrast, the subtle costumes of the grass dancers are relatively unadorned; they wear beadwork but no heavy headdresses. Women also compete, and the centrepiece of their costumes is the fringed and embroidered shawl that becomes a swirling prop in their graceful dances. Dresses are often decorated with cowrie shells and metal pieces that jingle with each step.

In recent years prize money has typically totaled well over $10,000, so competition is keen, with dancers studying each other's moves in a never-ending quest to come up with a new movement or interpretation that will add points for creativity. Dancers are judged on the precision of their movements and the rhythmic motion of their headdresses and bustles. No part of the costume should come loose. Dropping a feather can disqualify a dancer.

By Sunday afternoon the dancing reaches an athletic fervor, with young men doing athletic leaps and tumbles. The August heat doesn't seem to slow anybody down.

## *if you go*

**DIRECTIONS:** Manitoulin Island is reached by the Chi-Cheemaun ferry that sails between Tobermory (at the north end of Highway 6) and South Baymouth. The ferry is especially busy on that weekend, so it is wise to reserve by calling 1-800-265-3163, or to arrive well ahead of your planned sailing time. For ferry schedules call the Owen Sound Transportation Company at (519) 376-6601. The pow wow takes place at the village of Wikwemikong on the Manitoulin Island Indian Reserve at the eastern end of the island. Follow Highway 6 to the signs.

**SCHEDULE:** The annual pow wow takes place during the weekend of the August Civic Holiday. Schedules tend to be loose, but noon is generally the starting time for Saturday's grand parade.

**ADMISSION:** Daily tickets are on sale at the gate. Adults $5, students $4, children $2, preschoolers and seniors free.

Information: Call the Wikwemikong band office at (705) 859-3122.

**INFORMATION:** Call the Wikwemikong band office at (705) 859-3122.

**ACCOMMODATION:** Although this event is not widely publicized, people in the know often travel great distances to see it, and area motels are often solidly booked. The best bet to find accommodations is to call the island tourist office at (705) 368-3021. There are many rustic resorts, motels and bed-and-breakfast homes on the island.

**MAP REFERENCE:** The ferry to Manitoulin Island departs from Tobemory, 20.

## Dundurn Castle Candlelight Tours, Hamilton

Flickering candlelight seems to bring historic buildings to life. It softens hard edges, dims modern intrusions and lends a soft glow that transports visitors to the past. Hamilton's Dundurn Castle, the one-time home of politician Sir Allan MacNab, is at its best during the Christmas holidays when decked out in its Christmas finery, ready for festive and evocative evening tours.

Guests are welcomed into a grand hallway decorated with garlands of cedar by the local garden club, where they are greeted with a mug of mulled cider and a program of Christmas songs, fiddle or harp music. Costumed guides then lead the way through the castle, describing Victorian Christmas customs as they go. Especially in need of explanation is the unusual globe of greenery hanging in the front hall. This is the kissing bough, an old British tradition rich with symbolism. Within the sphere of evergreens a meter (3 1/2 feet) in diameter hang fruits and a mirrored ball, representing the sun and the planets of the solar system.

Since only small groups tour together (fifteen is the limit), the two-hour tour takes on a convivial spirit. Amid the red-brocade splendor of the drawing room, it is easy to imagine yourself a guest at one of the MacNab family's grand evenings. On a table sits a small spruce such as the one Queen Victoria introduced to England in the 1840s as acknowledgement of the royal family's Teutonic connections. By the 1850s, Christmas trees were beginning to catch on in Canada, and the MacNabs likely enjoyed a similar tree decorated with colourful cornucopias, crepe-paper Christmas crackers, baskets of fabric flowers, a dove made of traditional pierced paper, love boxes containing missives for the near and dear, gilded walnuts, and bunches of grapes made fron tissue paper. A gas light emits a warm glow from a clawfoot table, and the room looks set for the MacNabs to partake of a sherry or the wassail bowl.

In the library, guides talk a little about the laird of this lovely manor. Sir Allan MacNab was an aspiring politician, member of the Family Compact and famous for bringing the railway to Hamilton. When the house was designed he is said to have instructed the architect to design a home that would show his social position by dominating the landscape. Looking down over Burlington Bay, it certainly does command a view.

MacNab was one to command his guests' attention. In the emerald dining room, one gets a sense of the grandeur to which he aspired in his entertaining. The table is set with crystal, silver and linen for twenty people. At the centre is a towering epergne loaded with imported fruits. Pineapples, lemons and limes were the exotica of the day, available only to those who could afford the almost-prohibitive expense of transporting them to Canada. MacNab was no Scrooge when it came to entertaining, often offering an eight-course meal that would have taken the better part of a Christmas evening to consume. On the floor is a lead-lined wine sarcophagus for holding a dozen bottles of the best claret.

Family portraits that grace the dining room offer insights into the MacNabs. Sir Allan looks sturdy, like the old soldier he was, having received a knighthood for his part in the suppression of the 1837 rebellion. By contrast, his wife appears fragile; she suffered from tuberculosis. MacNab's wealth dwindled in his later years — one story circulates about how he talked workmen into accepting puppies as payment for labor — and little is left of the family silver. One remaining item, however, is a meat dish engraved with the severed head of a rival clan leader and the family motto, "Guneagal," meaning without fear.

Upstairs, daughters Minnie and

> *if you go*
>
> DIRECTIONS: Dundurn Castle is on York Blvd. in Hamilton. From the Queen Elizabeth Way take Highway 403 and follow the signs.
>
> SCHEDULE: Open daily year-round, noon to 4 p.m., June to Labour Day 10 a.m. to 4 p.m. Candlelight Evening tours are held on a dozen or more evenings from late November to mid-December.
>
> ADMISSION: Regular admission is adults $3.75, seniors $2.50, students $2.55, children $1.55. Tickets for the Candlelight tours cost approximately $8 and go on sale during the summer. Buy early because the tours are popular and always sell out.
>
> INFORMATION: Call (416) 522-5313
>
> MAP REFERENCE: 12

## Dundurn Castle Candlelight Tours

Sophia may have decorated their own tree with small toys and cookies. Children were becoming more involved in Christmas celebrations during the Victorian era, and party games were often an important part of the celebration. Rounds of charades were popular, but modern visitors may be shocked to learn about other MacNab family favourites, like Snap Dragon. In this game, currants were floated in a bowl of burning liquor, and players were expected to pluck out the blazing berries and pop them in their mouths.

No such fun and games for the servants down in the cellar. Christmas must have been a time of ceaseless toil as the cook struggled to keep the tables groaning and the scullery maid tackled mountains of dirty plates. Although the festive finery is spartan in the dungeonlike kitchens, the Christmas spirit seems warmest there as the spicy smell of mince tarts emanates from the brick oven. It's always the favourite stop on the candlelight tour, perhaps because of the delicacies served here, among them shortbread, Christmas cake, tarts and other fancies that seem to taste all the better for being baked in a wood-burning oven.

Even if you can't book a candlelight tour, it is well worth seeing Dundurn by daylight. Christmas decorations are on view from late November to the end of December. Christmas isn't the only celebration here. There are special events throughout the year, including a craft show in July.

## Stratford Festival Backstage Tours, Stratford

Each summer one of the best shows at the Stratford Festival is the cheapest. For $5, theatre lovers can take a fascinating Sunday morning tour of the Festival Theatre and catch a glimpse of the backstage work that makes the magic on stage.

Ushering a group into the empty theatre, a guide describes the history of the Stratford Festival, which held its first season in 1953 under the second-largest tent ever made in North America. (The largest tent belonged to the Ringling Brothers Circus.) When the prospering festival moved into a permanent building in 1957, the new theatre was designed to resemble the tent, with none of the 2,276 seats more than 22 m (66 feet) from the stage.

Based on the Elizabethan stage, the Festival Theatre's thrust stage juts into the audience area, which surrounds it in a 220-degree arc, thereby creating a set of problems actors don't normally encounter on the conventional proscenium stage. For instance, they cannot wait in the wings to watch the action for their cues, because they would be seen by the audience. Instead, video cameras cover the onstage action, which the actors view on backstage monitors. A guide shows how infrared lenses enable the technicians to see what is going on even when the theatre is in darkness, an important consideration since all set changes have to be made on a darkened stage.

Tunnels known as vomitoria lead into the darkened "underworld," which is the theatre's backstage space. This underworld is kept in murky darkness to prevent light from leaking onto the stage. Here shelves of spears and other props are handily laid out for actors as they make speedy entrances. Nine major entrances allow the large crowds and armies from Shakespeare's plays to pour onto the stage without confusion.

Trap doors perform a variety of functions, including holding smoke machines and serving as cellar doors and tombs. They also figure in some amusing anecdotes about the festival. My favourite is the story about the funeral that went awry in a 1957 production of *Hamlet*. One of the attendant monks got his cassock tangled in the ropes that were used

## Stratford Festival Backstage Tours

to lower Ophelia's body into the trap door grave, pulling him down into the grave with her. As the scene came to an end, the quick-thinking actors were left with no alternative but to bury the misguided monk alive with Ophelia.

Complicated costume changes can be made in less than a minute at the quick-change section where the pit-stop artists of the stage slip into costumes that may look as if they are held together by laces, hooks and period fasteners but are strategically sewn with strips of Velcro, enabling the most elaborate Elizabethan dresses to be ripped off and reassembled in seconds.

A tour of the wardrobe is like viewing the riches of the Orient. The fabric cage is filled with bolts of silk, a fabric preferred over other materials because it is both strong and easily dyed: all fabrics are printed, painted and dyed at the theatre. Shelves are piled high with boxes of costume adornments: rat tails, gold frogs, tinsel ribbon, corset stakes and bow ties. At the peak of the season between sixty and eighty people are at work attending to the costumes.

It is the detail work that is most fascinating: for example, when a character requires a costume that must look well worn, lighter shades of a dye must be painted along the seams to give the fabric a naturally aged look.

Everything from severed heads to a prince's throne is made in a prop room that epitomizes invention. Since sets are simple and there are no backdrops, the props are important in

---

### *if you go*

**DIRECTIONS:** Tours are held at the Festival Theatre, on Queen St. in Stratford. From Highway 401 exit onto Highway 8 west and follow it into Stratford. Follow the Festival Theatre signs.

**SCHEDULE:** Tours are offered every 15 minutes, from 9 to 10.30 a.m. on Sundays from early June to the end of the season.

**ADMISSION:** Tour tickets can be purchased in advance from the Festival Theatre box office and cost $5.

**INFORMATION:** For reservations and information call 364-8355 toll free from Toronto.

**MAP REFERENCE:** 18

evoking a setting. For example, an imitation topiary shrub suggests a formal garden, or a crude table suggests a tavern.

After seeing all backstage intricacies of the Festival Theatre, you'll feel ready to view the Sunday matinee with a newly appreciative eye.

## College Royal, Guelph

Tasting the foods of the future and watching live animal surgery are among the more offbeat activities in one of the most unusual university open houses in Canada. Because of its renowned agricultural and veterinary colleges, the University of Guelph has some particularly unusual displays in its annual open house, known as College Royal, held one weekend in mid-March.

Catering to the whole family, College Royal gives youngsters plenty of opportunities to see animals at close hand. Old dairy barns are turned into a petting farm where children can get close to pigs, sheep and calves. Singalong-style entertainments are usually organized for the barnyard bash.

The students, not the animals, are judged in a unique livestock show meant to groom the groomers. The pigs, sheep, cattle and horses in this competition are far from the perfect specimens one sees at the Royal Winter Fair, but poor colouring and shape don't matter here because the student trainers are judged for their ability in handling and grooming the animals. Hair on the beef cattle is carefully trimmed, and the beast is often bathed and groomed two or three times to prepare it for the show.

Visitors have a rare chance to tour the Ontario Veterinary College, where they may observe student vets in action. In the anatomy room, which contains skeletons of horses and cows and displays of organs, including a surprisingly large rumen of a cow. Students are usually on hand to talk about pet training, and visitors are invited to bring queries about pet problems.

Down the hall, second-year students examine dogs and cats, while in the surgery area, operations are performed for the public to watch, either from behind a window or on a video screen in a lecture room. In the large-animal wards visitors can see vets working on such typical cases as a horse with an infected hoof or cows with displaced stomachs.

The agricultural college typically features displays and demonstrations by such clubs as the Apiculturalists, who show visitors how queen bees are reared, or the Animal and Poultry Science Club, who show how meat and eggs are graded.

In addition to its veterinary and agricultural colleges, the university boasts the more conventional colleges, which stage some fairly unconventional displays. A highlight is always the chemistry department's "magic" show, with lots of smoke, fire and noise. Visitors can count on myriad campus clubs to stage a range of entertainments from medieval jousts to square dancing.

On a blustery March morning some of the most pleasant surroundings are the botany and horticulture greenhouses, where hibiscus are blooming and tropical fruits such as bananas, oranges and lemons are already growing on the trees.

## *if you go*

**DIRECTIONS:** The University of Guelph is in Guelph, north of Highway 401. From Highway 401 take Highway 6 north to Stone Rd., where you turn east. Go through the main entrance of the university (off Stone Rd.) and head straight for University Centre, where you can pick up a free map and brochure describing where all the events are held.

**SCHEDULE:** College Royal is usually held on the second weekend in March, Saturday 9 a.m. to 5 p.m., Sunday 11 a.m. to 5 p.m.

**ADMISSION:** Free.

**INFORMATION:** Call (519) 824-4120, extension 8366.

**MAP REFERENCE:** 17

# Calendar of Special Events

## january

**January 1**
**HOGMANAY**
Welcome the New Year in traditional Scottish style at historic Hutchison House in Peterborough, where the party is complete with traditional food and music to accompany the rituals. See page 67.

**Last Tuesday in January**
**CEDARENA BIRTHDAY PARTY**
A traditional skating party at the prettiest outdoor rink in Ontario, near Markham, with hot chocolate, doughnuts and spot prizes. See page 2.

## february

**First weekend in February**
**GROUNDHOG DAY WINTER CARNIVAL**
The Kortright Centre for Conservation in Kleinburg stages a fine winter carnival whatever the weather. Try traditional Native games like snow snakes or Inuit tug-of-war. See page 169.

## march

**Mid-March to mid-April**
**MAPLE SYRUP FESTIVALS**
Sugar bushes throughout Southern Ontario welcome visitors to see traditional and modern sap collecting and syrup making in the sugar shack. See page 109.

**Third Sunday in March**
**SWEET WATER DAY**
Maple syrup is prepared using traditional Native techniques and tools at Crawford Lake Conservation Area near Milton. Entertainment includes folk musicians and children's crafts. See page 38.

*april*

*Last weekend in April*
**FROG WATCHERS' HIKE**
Look for and listen to more than five species of frogs at the Mountsberg Wildlife Centre near Milton. See page 180.

*may*

*First weekend in May*
**FOUR WINDS KITE FESTIVAL**
A spectacular weekend of kite-flying and kite-making at the Kortright Centre for Conservation in Kleinburg, including the Canadian National Stunt Kite Championships. See page 169.

*First or second weekend in May*
**THE SPIRIT SOARS**
A day of flight features kites and turkey vultures soaring over the Niagara Escarpment, along with guided wildflower walks and Native planting ceremonies at Crawford Lake Indian Village and Conservation Area near Milton. See page 38.

*Sunday of Victoria Day weekend*
**PIONEER SHEEP AND WOOL CRAFT DAY**
A day of old-fashioned sheep and wool crafts including sheep-shearing, sheepdog demonstrations, dyeing, spinning and weaving at Lang Pioneer Village near Peterborough. See page 46.

*First weekend in June*
**BATTLE OF STONEY CREEK**
The historic battle that repelled American invaders during the War of 1812 is reenacted at Battlefield House. More than a dozen groups, including the local Lincoln Militia, provide a weekend of costumed drills, battles and other demonstrations. See page 52.

*First Sunday in June*
**SHARON TEMPLE FEAST DAY**
A day of traditional celebration at the historic temple near Newmarket features a Silver Band performing outdoors, plus demonstrations of pioneer crafts and cooking. See page 192.

*Father's Day*
**TRAPPERS' RENDEZVOUS**
Lang Pioneer Village near Peterborough stages a reenactment of a trappers' camp, when fur traders met and traded after a winter in the bush. See page 46.

*Father's Day Weekend*
**AIR SHOW**
Vintage warplanes as well as modern aircraft are flown at the Canadian Warplane Heritage Museum near Hamilton. See page 142.

*Last Sunday in June*
**LANG HERITAGE FESTIVAL**
This Canada Day celebration boasts Queen Victoria and her entourage, in addition to heritage music and pioneer crafts, at Lang Pioneer Village near Peterborough. See page 46.

*Late June*
**LEACOCK GARDEN PARTY**
A day of games, choirs, skits, magicians and fortune-tellers on the lawns of Stephen Leacock's summer home near Orillia. See page 78.

**july**

*July 1*
**CANADA DAY CELEBRATIONS**
An old-fashioned flag-waving party at the Ontario Agricultural Museum near Milton. See page 41.

*July 1*
**A GARDEN PARTY**
Join the fun at Woodside National Historical Site in Kitchener. See page 84.

*Mid-July*
**GREAT CANADIAN ANTIQUE TRACTOR FIELD DAYS**
This is your chance to see classic farm machinery wheezing and chugging at the Ontario Agricultural Museum near Milton. See page 41.

*One weekend in mid-July*
**MICROCOSM**
A craft show of nineteenth-century work typically includes demonstrations of marbleizing paper, chair-caning and furniture-making outdoors on the grounds of Dundurn Castle in Hamilton. See page 198.

*One Sunday in mid-July*
**FLOUR MILL DAY**
Horse and wagon rides and milling demonstrations at Lang Pioneer Village near Peterborough. See page 46.

*Mid-July to mid-August*
**CANDLELIGHT TOURS**
Fires and candles light the way in evening tours through historic Sainte-Marie Among the Hurons, near Midland. Afterward seventeenth-century desserts like blueberry cake are served in the café. Reservations are necessary. See page 57.

210   *calendar of special events*

*july*

*Occasional Sundays throughout summer*
**FAMILY GARDEN PARTY**
Bring your own picnic lunch to gracious Whitehern in Hamilton. The outdoor entertainment is typically a brass quintet or other popular music of the Edwardian era, games and activities for children and garden tours. Lemonade is served. See page 73.

*Last weekend in July*
**STEAM AND GAS SHOW**
Assorted engines wheeze, whirr and sputter into action at the Hamilton Museum of Steam and Technology. See page 55.

*august*

*Civic Holiday weekend*
**POW WOW**
Native people from across North America come to compete in this celebration of traditional Native dance, music and crafts at Wikwemikong on Manitoulin Island. See page 195.

*Sunday of Civic Holiday weekend*
**OTONABEE PIONEER CONTESTS DAY**
Old-fashioned fun includes a giant corn roast plus pioneer competitions for all ages including log-rolling, hay bale–throwing, log-sawing and greasy pole–climbing at Lang Pioneer Village near Peterborough. See page 46.

*Early August*
**COUNTRY QUILT FESTIVAL**
Ten days of quilt demonstrations and displays at the Ontario Agricultural Museum near Milton. See page 41.

*calendar of special events*

*august*

*Second weekend in August*
**FERGUS HIGHLAND GAMES**
An international event with traditional highland sports includes hammer throw and caber toss, plus Scottish dancers and pipe bands. Also Scottish-style entertainment throughout the town of Fergus. See page 186.

*Late August*
**FAMILY CORN FESTIVAL**
A weekend of corny celebrations features sweet cobs cooked by an antique steam engine, corn-husk crafts, children's activities and music at the Ontario Agricultural Museum near Milton. Children 10 and under admitted free. See page 41.

*Last Sunday in August*
**EVENING WITH THE BATS**
An instructional evening is spent catching bats in flight for close inspection at the Mountsberg Wildlife Centre near Milton. Registration required. See page 180.

**september**

*Labour Day Sunday*
**PIONEER CRAFT DAY**
A celebration of old-time skills with the craftspeople demonstrating straw-hat braiding to honey-separating at Lang Pioneer Village. See page 46.

*First Friday in September*
**SHARON TEMPLE ILLUMINATION**
The historic temple near Newmarket is lit with candlelight for a program of readings, choirs and a history talk. Tickets required. See page 192.

*First Sunday after Labour Day*
**INDIAN SUMMER**
A demonstration and sale of Native crafts is held at Crawford Lake Indian Village and Conservation Area near Milton, along with dancing and wagon rides to a scenic lookout. See page 38.

*Mid-September*
**HARVEST FESTIVAL AND FARMERS' MARKET**
Ontario Agricultural Museum in Milton. See page 41.

*Second or third Saturday in September*
**PIONEER FESTIVAL**
Lots of traditional Mennonite and Pennsylvania German foods are served at Black Creek Pioneer Village, in North York, along with an auction of handmade quilts, plus wagon rides, pioneer crafts and cooking. See page 190.

*Third Sunday in September*
**PIONEER APPLEFEST**
Apples are pressed for cider and made into apple fritters, apple dolls and other crafts at Lang Pioneer Village near Peterborough. See page 46.

*calendar of special events* **213**

**october**

*Thanksgiving weekend*
### HARVEST FESTIVAL
Demonstrations of pioneer skills, cider-pressing and home baking at the Sharon Temple, near Newmarket. See page 192.

*Sunday of Thanksgiving weekend*
### THANKSGIVING HARVEST FESTIVAL
Harvest demonstrations include threshing oats by steam engine and cider-making. A traditional "Bringing in the Sheaves" service is held in the historic church. All at Lang Pioneer Village near Peterborough. See page 46.

*Week leading up to Halloween*
### COBWEB PARTY
An unusual look at a Victorian Halloween celebration, with the parlour decorated in a tangle of strings. Candy-making and fortune-telling games are part of the fun at Woodside National Historic Site, near Kitchener. See page 84.

*Sunday before Halloween*
### ALL HALLOWS' EVE
Youngsters should wear costumes for this old-fashioned Halloween party, with activities like bobbing for apples and carving turnips, not pumpkins, into lanterns. At Barnum House Museum, Grafton. See page 75.

## november

*Late November through December*
### CANDLELIGHT EVENING TOURS
Dundurn Castle in Hamilton is lavishly decorated for evening tours by lantern and candlelight. Visitors taste seasonal treats while visiting the cellar kitchen. See page 198.

*Late November to early January*
### CHRISTMAS AT WOODSIDE
The boyhood home of William Lyon Mackenzie King is set up to show Victorian preparations for Christmas, including getting ready for the feast, making decorations in the library, garlands of greenery and a tree in the parlour. Music is performed on Sundays in the parlour. In Kitchener. See page 84.

## december

*December*
### CANDLELIGHT EVENINGS
On three special nights historic Battlefield House at Stoney Creek is lit by lanterns and candles for traditional crafts demonstrations. Old-fashioned Christmas goodies are served. See page 52.

*Mid-December*
### VICTORIAN CHRISTMAS FESTIVAL
Father Christmas visits Lang Pioneer Village near Peterborough for an afternoon of making decorations, music, skating on the millpond, sleigh rides, snowshoeing and a giant bonfire. See page 46.

*New Year's Eve*
### STEPHEN LEACOCK'S BIRTHDAY PARTY
Celebrate the author's birthday with an evening of musical and vocal entertainment. Snacks served and wine sold through a cash bar. In Orillia. See page 78.

*calendar of special events* 215

# Index

[Map Reference numbers in brackets]

## A

Aberfoyle Antique Market, Aberfoyle 154-55 [17]
Antique Market, Aberfoyle 154-55 [17]
Accommodations/Dining
  Bed & Breakfast Prince Edward County 7 [2]
  Benjamin's Restaurant and Inn, St. Jacobs 61 [16]
  Cataract Inn, Cataract 14-16 [11]
  Cove, The, Westport 24 [1]
  Elora Mill, The, Elora 34 [17]
  Gingerbread House, The, Elora 34 [17]
  Grandview Motel, The, Tobermory 134 [20]
  Guild Inn, The, Scarborough 25-27 [7]
  Jakobstettel Guest House, St. Jacobs 61 [16]
  Mallory House, The, Bloomfield 7 [2]
  Niagara-on-the-Lake Bed & Breakfast service 51 [13]
  Old Bridge Inn, Young's Point 119 [4]
  Tobermory Lodge, The, Tobermory 134 [20]
  Union Hotel, Normandale 124-25 [14]
  Westport bed and breakfasts 23 [1]
  Wheelhouse, The, Picton (restaurant) 92 [2]
African Lion Safari and Game Farm, Rockton 160-62 [12]
Alexander Graham Bell Homestead, Brantford 81-83 [15]
Animals
  African Lion Safari and Game Farm, Rockton 160-62 [12]
  Arboretum Nature Centre, Guelph 178-79 [17]
  College Royal, Guelph 204-5 [17]
  Kortright Centre for Conservation, Kleinburg 169-71 [8]
  Mountsberg Wildlife Centre, Milton 180-81 [11]
  Ontario Vacation Farms 20-22
  Royal Botanical Gardens 175-77 [12]
  Wye Marsh Wildlife Centre, Midland 172-74 [9]
Antiques
  Aberfoyle Antique Market, Aberfoyle 154-55 [17]
  Alton and Belfountain, near Caledon Hills Provincial Park 14-16 [11]
Aquafarms, Feversham 111-12 [19]
Arboretum Nature Centre, Guelph 178-79 [17]
Archaeology
  Crawford Lake Indian Village and Conservation Area, Milton 38-40 [11]
  Petroglyphs Provincial Park, Bancroft 44-45 [4]
Arkona
  Rock Glen Conservation Area 8-10 [22]

## B

Balloon Rides
  Cross Canada Balloons, Uxbridge 28-30 [6]
Bancroft
  Petroglyphs Provincial Park 44-45 [4]
Barnum House, Grafton 75-77 [3]

*index* 217

# Index

Barry's Bay
  Madawaska Kanu Centre 31-33 [1]
Battlefield House, Stoney Creek 52-54 [12]
Beekeeping
  Arboretum Nature Centre, Guelph 179 [17]
  Kortright Centre for Conservation, Kleinburg 169-71 [8]
Bicycling
  Jakobstettel Guest House, St. Jacobs 61 [16]
Bird-watching
  Arboretum Nature Centre, Guelph 178-79 [17]
  Bluffers Park, Scarborough 25-27 [7]
  Caledon Hills Provincial Park, Cataract 14-15 [11]
  Jack Miner Sanctuary, Kingsville, and Point Pelee National Park, Leamington 166-68 [22]
  Kortright Centre for Conservation, Kleinburg 169-71 [8]
  Kortright Waterfowl Park, Guelph 163-65 [17]
  Mountsberg Wildlife Centre, Milton 180-81 [11]
  Rock Glen Conservation Area, Arkona 8-10 [22]
  Royal Botanical Gardens, Hamilton 175-77 [12]
  Sandbanks Provincial Park, Picton 4-6 [2]
  Turkey Point Provincial Park, Port Dover 125 [14]
  Wye Marsh Wildlife Centre, Midland 172-74 [9]
Black Creek Pioneer Village Pioneer Festival, North York 190-91 [7]
Bluffers Park and The Guild Inn, Scarborough 25-27 [7]
Brant [15]
  Alexander Graham Bell Homestead, Brantford 81-83
Brantford
  Alexander Graham Bell Homestead 81-83 [15]
Bruce [20]
  Bruce Peninsula National Park, Tobermory 17-19
  Dorcas Bay Nature Reserve, Tobermory 182-83
  Flowerpot Island, Tobermory 132-34
  Wikwemikong Pow Wow, Manitoulin Island 195-97
Bruce Peninsula National Park, Tobermory 17-19 [20]
Bruce's Mill Conservation Area Sugar Bush, Stouffville 108-10 [8]
Burlington
  Burlington History Gallery 94 [11]
  Joseph Brant Museum 93-95 [11]

**C**
Caledon Hills Provincial Park and Cataract Inn, Cataract 14-15 [11]
Camping
  Cyprus Lake Campground, Bruce Peninsula National Park, Tobermory 17-19 [20]
  Flowerpot Island, Tobermory 134 [20]
  Frontenac Provincial Park, Westport 23 [1]
  Gould Lake, Rideau Trail 23 [1]
  Madawaska Kanu Centre, Barry's Bay 32 [1]
  Sandbanks Provincial Park, Picton 7 [2]
  Tobermory 183 [20]

Canadian Automotive Museum, The, Oshawa 148-50 [6]
Canadian Warplane Heritage Museum, Hamilton 142-44 [12]
Candlelight Tours
  Battlefield House, Stoney Creek 52, 215 [12]
  Dundurn Castle Candlelight Tours, Hamilton 198-99 [12]
  Sainte-Marie Among the Hurons, Midland 57-59 [9]
Canoeing
  Madawaska Kanu Centre, Barry's Bay 31-33 [1]
  Wye Marsh Wildlife Centre, Midland 174 [9]
Cataract
  Caledon Hills Provincial Park and Cataract Inn 14-16 [11]
Cedarena, Markham 2-3 [8]
Château des Charmes, St. Davids 107 [13]
Children's Activities
  African Lion Safari and Game Farm, Rockton 160-62 [12]
  Arboretum Nature Centre, Guelph 179 [17]
  Black Creek Pioneer Village Pioneer Festival, North York (wagon rides) 190-91 [7]
  Bruce's Mill Conservation Area Sugar Bush, Stouffville 108-10 [8]
  Canadian Automotive Museum, The, Oshawa 148-50 [6]
  Canadian Warplane Heritage Museum, Hamilton 142-44 [12]
  Carousel, Lakeside Park, Port Dalhousie 128 [13]
  Cedarena, Markham (skating) 2, 207 [8]
  Chudleigh's Apple Farm, Milton 98-100 [8]
  College Royal, Guelph 204-5 [17]
  Crawford Lake Indian Village and Conservation Area, Milton
    (Indian Summer, maple-syrup making, wagon rides) 38, 207-8, 213 [11]
  Cullen Gardens and Miniature Village, Whitby 151-53 [6]
  Devins Orchards, Toronto 98-100 [8]
  Kleinburg Doll Museum, Kleinburg 145-47 [8]
  Kortright Centre for Conservation, Kleinburg
    (kite-making, kite-flying, Winter Carnival) 169, 207, 208 [8]
  Kortright Waterfowl Park, Guelph 163-65 [17]
  Lang Pioneer Village, Peterborough
    (Flour Mill Day, Otonobee Pioneer Contests Day, Pioneer Applefest,
    South Lake School, Victorian Christmas Festival) 46, 210, 211, 213, 215 [4]
  Mountsberg Wildlife Centre, Milton
    (Frog Watchers' Hike, Evening with the Bats) 180, 208, 212 [11]
  Museum and Archives of Games, Waterloo 156-57 [16]
  Ontario Agricultural Museum, Milton (Family Corn Festival) 41, 212 [11]
  Ontario Vacation Farms 20-22
  Pleasure Valley, Claremont
    (rollerskating, wagon rides, playground, petting zoo, water slides) 11-13 [6]
  Sandbanks Provincial Park, Picton (environmental lessons, Native pottery-making) 4-6 [2]
  Stephen Leacock Home, Orillia (Leacock Garden Party) 78, 209 [9]
  Whitehern, Hamilton (Family Garden Party) 73, 211 [12]
  Woodside National Historic Site, Kitchener (Cobweb Party, Christmas) 84, 214 [16]
Chudleigh's Apple Farm 98-100 [11]

*index* **219**

# Index

Claremont
　Pleasure Valley 11-13 [6]
Cobourg
　Barnum House Museum 75-77 [3]
　Victoria Hall 77 [3]
College Royal, Guelph 204-5 [17]
Collingwood
　Aquafarms, Feversham 111-12 [19]
Crafts
　Meeting Place, The, St. Jacobs 60-62 [16]
Crawford Lake Indian Village and Conservation Area, Milton 38-40 [11]
Cross Canada Balloons, Uxbridge 28-30 [6]
Cross-country Skiing
　Bruce's Mill Conservation Area Sugar Bush, Stouffville 108-10 [8]
　Caledon Hills Provincial Park 14-15 [11]
　Chudleigh's Apple Farm, Milton 100 [11]
　Crawford Lake Indian Village and Conservation Area, Milton 38- 40 [11]
　Jakobstettel Guest House, St. Jacobs 61 [16]
　Mountsberg Wildlife Centre, Milton 180-81 [11]
　Pleasure Valley, Claremont 11-13 [6]
　Rideau Trail, Westport 23-25 [1]
　Turkey Point Provincial Park, Port Dover 125 [14]
Cruises/Boat Rides
　Chi-Cheemun ferry, Tobermory to Manitoulin Island 133-34 [20]
　Historic Naval and Military Establishments, Penetanguishene,
　　Sailor's Sunset cruises 130 [9]
　*Island Princess*, Orillia 80 [9]
　Lift Lock Cruises, Peterborough 118 [4]
　*Maid of the Mist*, Niagara Falls 120-22 [13]
　*Peggy Jane*, Port Dover Harbour Museum, Port Dover 123 [14]
　R.M.S. *Segwun*, Gravenhurst 114-16 [10]
　M.V. *Seaview III*, Little Tub Harbour, Tobermory 132 [20]
Cullen Gardens and Miniature Village, Whitby 151-53 [6]

**D**
Devins Orchards, Toronto 98-99 [8]
Dogsledding
　Lang Pioneer Village, Peterborough 46-48 [4]
　Dorcas Bay Nature Reserve, Tobermory 182-83 [20]
Dufferin, Wellington [17]
　Aberfoyle Antique Market, Aberfoyle 154-55
　Arboretum Nature Centre, Guelph 178-79
　College Royal, Guelph 204-5
　Elora Gorge, Elora 34-35
　Fergus Highland Games, Fergus 186-89
　Kortright Waterfowl Park, Guelph 163-65
　Dundurn Castle Candlelight Tours, Hamilton 198-99 [12]

Durham, Victoria [6]
Canadian Automotive Museum, The, Oshawa 148-50
Cross Canada Balloons, Uxbridge 28-30
Cullen Gardens and Miniature Village, Whitby 151-53
Parkwood, Oshawa 87-89
Pleasure Valley, Claremont 11-13
Richters Herbs, Stouffville 103-5

## E

Eastern Ontario [1]
Madawaska Kanu Centre, Barry's Bay 31-33
Rideau Trail, Westport 23-24
Elora
Elora Gorge Conservation Area 34-35 [17]

## F

Farmers' Markets
Black Creek Pioneer Village Pioneer Festival, North York 190-91 [7]
Fergus 188 [17]
Ontario Agricultural Museum, Milton (mid-September) 43 [11]
St. Jacobs Farmers' Market and Flea Market 62 [16]
Waterloo County Farmers' Market 62 [16]
Fathom Five National Marine Park, Tobermory 133 [20]
Fergus
Fergus Highland Games 186-89 [17]
Feversham
Aquafarms 111-12 [19]
Fishing
Aquafarms, Feversham 111-12 [19]
Bluffers Park, Scarborough 25-27 [7]
Madawaska Kanu Centre, Barry's Bay 32 [1]
Flowerpot Island, Tobermory 132-34 [20]
Foley Mountain Conservation Area 24 [1]
Fort George National Historic Park, Niagara-on-the-Lake 49-51 [13]
Fossils
Flowerpot Island, Tobermory 133 [20]
Rock Glen Conservation Area, Arkona 8-10 [22]

## G

Geology
Crawford Lake Indian Village and Conservation Area, Milton, 38-40 [11]
Petroglyphs Provincial Park, Bancroft 44-45 [4]
Grafton
Barnum House Museum 75-77 [3]
Gravenhurst
Norman Bethune Memorial House 64-66 [10]
R.M.S. *Segwun*, 114-16 [10]
Grey [19]
Aquafarms, Feversham 111-12

# Index

Guelph
  Arboretum Nature Centre 178-79 [17]
  College Royal 204-5 [17]
  Kortright Waterfowl Park 163-65 [17]
  Ontario Electric Railway Museum 136-38 [11]

Haldimand-Norfolk [14]
  Port Dover Harbour Museum, The, Port Dover 123-25
  Turkey Point Provincial Park, Port Dover 125
Halton, Peel [11]
  Burlington History Gallery, Burlington 94
  Caledon Hills Provincial Park and Cataract Inn, Cataract 14-16
  Crawford Lake Indian Village and Conservation Area, Milton 38-40
  Joseph Brant Museum, Burlington 93-95
  Mountsberg Wildlife Centre, Milton 180-81
  Ontario Agricultural Museum, Milton 41-43
  Ontario Electric Railway Museum, Guelph 136-38
Hamilton
  Canadian Warplane Heritage Museum 142-44 [12]
  Dundurn Castle Candlelight Tours 198-99 [12]
  Hamilton Museum of Steam and Technology, The 55-56 [12]
  Royal Botanical Gardens 175-77 [12]
Hamilton Museum of Steam and Technology, The, Hamilton 55-56 [12]
Hamilton, Wentworth [12]
  African Lion Safari and Game Farm, Rockton 160-62
  Battlefield House, Stoney Creek 52-54
  Canadian Warplane Heritage Museum, Hamilton 142-44
  Dundurn Castle Candlelight Tours, Hamilton 198-99
  Hamilton Museum of Steam and Technology, The, Hamilton 55-56
  Royal Botanical Gardens, Hamilton 175-77
  Whitehern, Hamilton 73-74
Herbs
  Richters Herbs, Stouffville 103-4 [6]
  Royal Botanical Gardens, Hamilton 175-77 [12]
Hiking/Nature Walks
  Arboretum Nature Centre, Guelph 178-79 [17]
  Bruce Peninsula National Park, Tobermory 17-19 [20]
  Caledon Hills Provincial Park 14-15 [11]
  Crawford Lake Indian Village and Conservation Area, Milton 38-40 [11]
  Dorcas Bay Nature Reserve, Tobermory 182-83 [20]
  Elora Gorge, Elora 34-35 [17]
  Flowerpot Island, Tobermory 133 [20]
  Jakobstettel Guest House, St. Jacobs 61 [16]
  Kortright Centre for Conservation, Kleinburg 169-71 [8]
  Madawaska Kanu Centre, Barry's Bay 32 [1]
  Mountsberg Wildlife Centre, Milton 180-81 [11]
  Petroglyphs Provincial Park, Bancroft 45 [4]

Pleasure Valley, Claremont 11-13 [6]
Rideau Trail, Westport 23-25 [1]
Royal Botanical Gardens, Hamilton 175-77 [12]
Sandbanks Provincial Park, Cedar Sands Nature Trail, Picton 4-6 [2]
Turkey Point Provincial Park, Port Dover 125 [14]
Wye Marsh Wildlife Centre, Midland 172-74 [9]
Historic Naval and Military Establishments, Penetanguishene 129- 31 [9]
Horseback Riding
 Pleasure Valley, Claremont 11-13 [6]
Horse-drawn Wagon Rides
 Bruce's Mills Conservation Area Sugar Bush, Stouffville 109 [8]
Hutchison House Museum, Peterborough 67-69 [4]

# I

Inniskillin (winery) 107 [13]

# J

Jack Miner Sanctuary, Kingsville, and Point Pelee National Park, Leamington 166-68 [22]
Joseph Brant Museum, Burlington 93-95 [11]

# K

Kayaking
 Madawaska Kanu Centre, Barry's Bay 31-33 [1]
 Sandbanks Provincial Park, Picton 4-6 [2]
Kleinburg
 Kleinburg Doll Museum 145-47 [8]
 Kortright Centre for Conservation 169-71 [8]
Kingsville
 Jack Miner Sanctuary 166-68 [22]
Kitchener
 Woodside National Historic Site 84-86 [16]
Kortright Centre for Conservation, Kleinburg 169-71 [8]
Kortright Waterfowl Park, Guelph 163-65 [17]

# L

Lake on the Mountain Conservation Area, Picton 92 [2]
Lang Pioneer Village, Peterborough 46-48 [4]
Laura Secord Homestead, Queenston 70-72 [13]
Leamington
 Point Pelee National Park 166-68 [22]
Lift Lock, Peterborough 117-19 [4]

# Index

Lincoln, Welland [13]
  Château des Charmes, St. Davids 107
  Fort George National Historic Park, Niagara-on-the-Lake 49-51
  Inniskillin (winery) 107
  Laura Secord Homestead, Queenston 70-72
  *Maid of the Mist*, Niagara Falls 120-22
  Niagara Apothecary Museum, Niagara-on-the-Lake 139-41
  Niagara Helicopters Ltd., Niagara Falls 121
  Reif (winery) 107
  Stoney Ridge Cellars 105
  Welland Canal Lock No 3 Viewing Complex, St. Catharines 126-28
  Wiley Bros. Ltd., St. Catharines 106

Macaulay Heritage Park, Picton 90-92 [2]
*Maid of the Mist*, Niagara Falls 120-22 [13]
Madawaska Kanu Centre, Barry's Bay 31-33 [1]
Manitoulin Island
  Wikwemikong Pow Wow 195-97 [20]
Maple Sugar Bushes
  Black Creek Pioneer Village, North York 110 [7]
  Bruce's Mill Conservation Area Sugar Bush, Stouffville 108-10 [8]
  Crawford Lake Indian Village and Conservation Area, Milton 38-40, 110 [11]
  Kortright Centre for Conservation, Kleinburg 110 [8]
  Mountsberg Wildlife Centre, Milton 181 [11]
  Royal Botanical Gardens, Hamilton 110, 175-77 [12]
  Wye Marsh Wildlife Centre, Midland 174 [9]
Markham
  Cedarena 2-3 [8]
Meeting Place, The, St. Jacobs 60-62 [16]
Metropolitan Toronto [7]
  Black Creek Pioneer Village Pioneer Festival, 190-91
  Bluffers Park and The Guild Inn, Scarborough 25-27
Midland
  Sainte-Marie Among the Hurons 57-59 [9]
  Wye Marsh Wildlife Centre 172-74 [9]
Milton
  Chudleigh's Apple Farm 98-100 [11]
  Crawford Lake Indian Village and Conservation Area 38-40 [11]
  Mountsberg Wildlife Centre 180-81 [11]
  Ontario Agricultural Museum 41-43 [11]
Mountsberg Wildlife Centre, Milton 180-81 [11]
Museum and Archives of Games, Waterloo 156-57 [16]
Museums
  Alexander Graham Bell Homestead, Brantford 81-83 [15]
  Barnum House Museum, Grafton 75-77 [3]
  Battlefield House, Stoney Creek 52-54 [12]
  Black Creek Pioneer Village, North York 190-91 [7]
  Bluffers Park and The Guild Inn, Scarborough 25-27 [7]

Burlington History Gallery, Burlington 94 [11]
Canadian Automotive Museum, The, Oshawa 148-50 [6]
Canadian Warplane Heritage Museum, Hamilton 142-44 [12]
Dundurn Castle, Hamilton 198-99 [12]
Fort George National Historic Park, Niagara-on-the-Lake, 49-52 [13]
Hamilton Museum of Steam and Technology, The, Hamilton 55-56 [12]
Historic Naval and Military Establishments, Penetanguishene 129-31 [9]
Hutchison House Museum, Peterborough 67-69 [4]
Joseph Brant Museum, Burlington 93-95 [11]
Kleinburg Doll Museum, Kleinburg 145-47 [8]
Lang Pioneer Village, Peterborough 46-48 [4]
Laura Secord Homestead, Queenston 70-72 [13]
Macaulay Heritage Park, Picton 90-92 [2]
Meeting Place, The, St. Jacobs 60-62 [16]
Museum and Archives of Games, Waterloo 156-57 [16]
Niagara Apothecary Museum, Niagara-on-the-Lake 139-41 [13]
Niagara Historical Society Museum, Niagara-on-the-Lake 72 [13]
Norman Bethune Memorial House, Gravenhurst 64-66 [10]
Ontario Agricultural Museum, Milton 41-43 [11]
Ontario Electric Railway Museum, Guelph 136-38 [11]
Parkwood, Oshawa 87-89 [6]
Port Dover Harbour Museum, Port Dover 123-25 [14]
Rock Glen Conservation Area, Arkona 10 [22]
St. Catharines Historical Museum, St. Catharines 126 [13]
Sainte-Marie Among the Hurons, Midland 57-59 [9]
Sharon Temple, Newmarket 192-94 [8]
Spencer Clark Collection of Historic Architecture, Scarborough 26 [7]
Stephen Leacock Home, Orillia 78-79 [9]
Welland Canal Lock No 3 Viewing Complex and Information Centre
    and Museum, St. Catharines 126-28 [13]
Whitehern, Hamilton 73-74 [12]
Woodside National Historic Site, Kitchener 84-87 [16]
Muskoka [10]
  Norman Bethune House, Gravenhurst 64-66
  R.M.S. *Segwun*, Gravenhurst 114-16

Native Activities
  Wikwemikong Pow Wow, Manitoulin Island 195-97 [20]
Native Artifacts
  Rock Glen Conservation Area, Arkona 10 [22]
Native Villages
  Crawford Lake Indian Village and Conservation Area, Milton 38-40 [11]
  Sainte-Marie Among the Hurons, Midland 57-59 [9]
Newmarket
  Sharon Temple Feast Days and Illumination 192-94 [8]
  Niagara Apothecary Museum, Niagara-on-the-Lake 137-39 [13]

# Index

Niagara Falls
  *Maid of the Mist* 120-22 [13]
  Niagara Helicopters Ltd. 121 [13]
  Niagara Historical Society Museum, Niagara-on-the-Lake 72 [13]
Niagara-on-the-Lake
  Fort George National Historic Park 49-51 [13]
  Laura Secord Homestead, Queenston 70-72 [13]
  Niagara Apothecary Museum 139-41 [13]
  Niagara Historical Society Museum 72 [13]
  Niagara-on-the-Lake Bed and Breakfast service 51 [13]
Norman Bethune Memorial House, Gravenhurst 64-66 [10]
Northumberland [3]
  Barnum House, Grafton 75-77
  Victoria Hall, Cobourg 77

Ontario Agricultural Museum, Milton 41-43 [11]
Ontario Electric Railway Museum, Guelph 136-38 [11]
Ontario Vacation Farm Association 21
Orillia
  *Island Princess* 80 [9]
  Stephen Leacock Home 78-79 [9]
Oshawa
  Canadian Automotive Museum, The 148-50 [6]
  Parkwood 87-89 [6]

Parkwood, Oshawa 87-89 [6]
Penetanguishene
  Historic Naval and Military Establishments 129-31 [9]
Perth, Oxford [18]
  Stratford Festival Backstage Tours, Stratford 201-3
Peterborough [4]
  Hutchison House Museum 67-69
  Lang Pioneer Village 46-48
  Lift Lock 117-19
  Petroglyphs Provincial Park, Bancroft 44-45
Petroglyphs Provincial Park, Bancroft 44-45 [4]
Pick-Your-Own Report 100 [8]
  Ontario Berry Growers' Hotline 100 [8]
Picton
  Lake on the Mountain Conservation Area 92 [2]
  Macaulay Heritage Park 90-92 [2]
  Sandbanks Provincial Park 4-7 [2]
Pioneer Villages
  Black Creek Pioneer Village, North York 190-92 [7]
  Lang Pioneer Village, Peterborough 46-48 [4]
  Pleasure Valley, Claremont 11-13 [6]

Port Dalhousie
  Carousel, Lakeside Park 128 [13]
  Port Weller Dry Docks 127 [13]
  Royal Canadian Henley Regatta 128 [13]
Port Dover
  Turkey Point Provincial Park 125 [14]
  Port Dover Harbour Museum, Port Dover 123-25 [14]
Port Weller Dry Docks 127 [13]
Prince Edward [2]
  Lake on the Mountain Conservation Area, Picton 92
  Macaulay Heritage Park, Picton 90-92
  Sandbanks Provincial Park, Picton 4-5

## Q

Queenston
  Laura Secord Homestead 70-72 [13]

## R

Reif (winery) 107 [13]
Richters Herbs, Stouffville 103-4 [6]
Rideau Trail, Westport 23-24 [1]
R.M.S. *Segwun*, Gravenhurst 114-16 [10]
Rock Glen Conservation Area, Arkona 8-10 [22]
Rockton
  African Lion Safari and Game Farm 160-62 [12]
Rollerskating
  Pleasure Valley, Claremont 11-13 [6]
Royal Botanical Gardens, Hamilton 175-77 [12]
Royal Canadian Henley Regatta, Port Dalhousie 128 [13]

## S

Sailboarding, Sailing, Kayaking
  Sandbanks Provincial Park, Picton 4-6 [2]
St. Catharines
  St. Catharines Historical Museum 126 [13]
  Welland Canal Lock No 3 Viewing Complex 126-28 [13]
St. Jacobs
  Meeting Place, The 60-62 [16]
Sainte-Marie Among the Hurons, Midland 57-59 [9]
Sandbanks Provincial Park, Picton 4-6 [2]
Scuba Diving
  Flowerpot Island, Tobermory 132 [20]
Sharon Temple Feast Days and Illumination, Newmarket 192-94 [8]

*index* 227

# Index

Simcoe [9]
   Historic Naval and Military Establishments, Penetanguishene 129-31
   *Island Princess*, Orillia 80
   Sainte-Marie Among the Hurons, Midland 57-59
   Stephen Leacock Home, Orillia 78-79
   Wye Marsh Wildlife Centre, Midland 172-74
Skating
   Bruce's Mill Conservation Area Sugar Bush, Stouffville 109 [8]
   Cedarena, Markham 2-3 [8]
Skiing
   Elora Gorge Conservation Area, Elora 35 [17]
Sleigh Rides
   Pleasure Valley, Claremont 11-13 [6]
Snowshoeing
   Arboretum Nature Centre, Guelph 178-79 [17]
   Caledon Hills Provincial Park 14-15 [11]
South Western Ontario [22]
   Jack Miner Sanctuary, Kingsville, and Point Pelee National Park, Leamington 166-68
   Rock Glen Conservation Area, Arkona 8-10
   Spencer Clark Collection of Historic Architecture, Scarborough 26 [7]
   Stephen Leacock Home, Orillia, 78-79 [9]
Stoney Creek
   Battlefield House 52-54 [12]
   Stoney Ridge Cellars, Stoney Ridge 105 [13]
Stouffville
   Bruce's Mill Conservation Area Sugar Bush 108-10 [8]
   Richters Herbs 103-5 [6]
Stratford
   Stratford Festival Backstage Tours 201-3 [18]

Tobermory
   Bruce Peninsula National Park 17-19 [20]
   Dorcas Bay Nature Reserve 182-83 [20]
   Fathom Five National Marine Park 133 [20]
   Flowerpot Island 132-34 [20]
   M.V. *Seaview III*, Little Tub Harbour 132 [20]
Toronto Area
   Black Creek Pioneer Village, North York 190-91 [7]
   Bluffers Park and The Guild Inn, Scarborough 25-27 [7]
   Bruce's Mill Conservation Area Sugar Bush, Stouffville 108-10 [8]
   Caledon Hills Provincial Park 14-15 [11]
   Cedarena, Markham 2-3 [8]
   Chudleigh's Apple Farm, Milton 98-100 [11]
   Crawford Lake Indian Village and Conservation Area, Milton 180-81 [11]
   Cross Canada Balloons, Uxbridge 28-39 [6]
   Devins Orchards, Toronto 98-100 [8]
   Kleinburg Doll Museum, Kleinburg 145-47 [8]

Kortright Centre for Conservation, Kleinburg 169-71 [8]
Mountsberg Wildlife Centre, Milton 180-81 [11]
Ontario Agricultural Museum, Milton 43 [11]
Pleasure Valley, Claremont 11-13 [6]
Richters Herbs, Stouffville 103-4 [6]
Sharon Temple Feast Days and Illumination, Newmarket 192-94 [8]
Toy Collections
  Black Creek Pioneer Village, North York 191 [7]
  Kleinburg Doll Museum, Kleinburg 145-47 [8]
Traditional Dancing
  Fergus Highland Games, Fergus 186-89 [17]
  Wikwemikong Pow Wow, Manitoulin Island 195-97 [20]
Turkey Point Provincial Park, Port Dover 125 [14]
Tyrone Mill, Bowmanville 101 [6]

## V

Victoria Hall, Cobourg 77 [3]
Vintage Vehicles
  Canadian Automotive Museum, The, Oshawa 148-50 [6]
  Canadian Warplane Heritage Museum, Hamilton 142-44 [12]
  Ontario Agricultural Museum, Milton 41-43 [11]
  Ontario Electric Railway Museum, Guelph 136-38 [11]

## W

Water Playground
  African Lion Safari and Game Farm, Rockton 162 [12]
  Pleasure Valley, Claremont 11-13 [6]
Waterloo [16]
  Meeting Place, The, St. Jacobs 60-62
  Museum and Archives of Games, Waterloo 156-57
  Woodside National Historic Site, Kitchener 84-86
Welland Canal Lock No 3 Viewing Complex, St. Catharines 126-28 [13]
Westport
  Rideau Trail 23-25 [1]
Whitby
  Cullen Gardens and Miniature Village 151-53 [6]
Whitehern, Hamilton 73-74 [12]
Wikwemikong Pow Wow, Manitoulin Island 195-97 [20]
Wiley Bros. Ltd., St. Catharines 106 [16]
Wildflowers
  Arboretum Nature Centre, Guelph 178-79 [17]
  Crawford Lake Indian Village and Conservation Area, Milton 40 [11]
  Dorcas Bay Nature Reserve, Tobermory 182-83 [20]
  Kortright Centre for Conservation, Kleinburg 169-71 [8]
  Wye Marsh Wildlife Centre, Midland 172-74 [9]
Woodside National Historic Site, Kitchener 84-86 [16]
Wye Marsh Wildlife Centre, Midland 172-74 [9]

*index* **229**

# Index

York [8]
 Bruce's Mill Conservation Area Sugar Bush, Stouffville 108-10
 Cedarena, Markham 2-3
 Devins Orchards, Toronto 98-100
 Kleinburg Doll Museum, Kleinburg 145-47
 Kortright Centre for Conservation, Kleinburg 169-71
 Sharon Temple Feast Days and Illumination, Newmarket 192-94